TRADITIONAL
GIFTS

TRADITIONAL GIFTS

VINNY LEE

SPECIAL PHOTOGRAPHY BY
PIA TRYDE

CONRAN OCTOPUS

PROJECT EDITOR	Joanna Bradshaw
EDITOR	Dina Medland
EDITORIAL ASSISTANT	Sally Poole
ART EDITOR	Meryl Lloyd
DESIGNER	Alison Shackleton
PICTURE RESEARCH	Jessica Walton
PRODUCTION	Jackie Kernaghan
SPECIAL PHOTOGRAPHY	Pia Tryde
ART DIRECTOR OF SPECIAL PHOTOGRAPHY	Georgina Rhodes
STYLIST	Jane Newdick

First published in 1990 by Conran Octopus Limited
37 Shelton Street, London WC2H 9HN

Copyright © 1990 Conran Octopus Limited

British Library Cataloguing in Publication Data
Lee, Vinny
    Traditional gifts
    1. Handicrafts
    I Title
745.5

ISBN 1-85029-268-X

Typeset by Tradespools Limited
Printed and bound in Hong Kong

CONTENTS

INTRODUCTION

THERE ARE MANY OCCASIONS WHEN gifts are given and exchanged. Some gifts mark an annual event such as a birthday or Christmas, while others are given more spontaneously, to express gratitude or appreciation.

The emphasis of present-day gift-giving too often lies on the cost and availability of an object, which can overshadow the real and original sentiments intended to accompany the gift. Contemporary presents are often predictable – a factory-made box of chocolates is bought, wrapped and dispatched in haste, with little thought given to what may be appropriate for either the recipient or the occasion.

This book looks at the preparation of traditional hand-crafted gifts, as well as the histories and legends with which they are associated, bringing the customs of the past up to date with practical projects that show how to make gifts unique.

A LITTLE GIFT BY FRIENDSHIP'S HAND CONFERRED,
IS OFTEN TO THE COSTLIEST GEM PREFERRED.

Anon

FLOWERS AND SAMPLERS

(Above) Flowers as gifts are probably one of the oldest and most universally acceptable options.
(Right) Samplers, like this Danish example of 1754 from the Dansk Folk museum, recorded domestic history as accurately as written manuscripts.

GIVING AND RECEIVING

Traditionally, a gift would have been made by the person giving it. No matter how small or inexpensive the gift was, it carried with it a personal and emotional value that could not be bought with money.

Family events, such as an engagement or christening have always been celebrated with the bestowing of hand-made gifts, most commonly food and clothes. The giving of food and drink – the substances of life – is an ancient custom that can be traced back beyond biblical times. Even the most humble of these domestic offerings can be made unique with a little extra effort and imagination, if not in the ingredients then at least in the preparation and presentation.

In the past, among poor rural communities, new arrivals to a country area would be greeted by their neighbours. Often a welcome ring made with herbs and grasses would be plaited and presented to the new people as a symbol of good luck. Alternatively, as a gesture of friendship, neighbours might have visited and delivered a bottle of their own freshly-made fruit cordial or lemonade.

More elaborate gifts could take months to prepare, truly deserving to be called 'labours of love'. Finely stitched tapestry samplers, personally inscribed embroidered items, historically patterned seafarers' jumpers and bridal gifts of fine lace all hark back to a time when a gift was a major undertaking, involving time and effort rather than a swift dash to the stationery shop. Nowadays, a date in the diary or television advertising reminds us that it is time to go out and buy gifts again.

LABOURS OF LOVE

Some of the most valued gifts are those that pass between lovers, whether it is a lasting token such as a ring, or an ephemeral but significant gesture such as a single rose. It is frequently the emotional message of a romantic gift that is the important element.

Flowers that are personally selected and arranged are so much more beautiful and original than a clichéd florist's bouquet. For a meaningful arrangement,

BE MY VALENTINE

Cupid, the son of Venus the goddess of love, adopted many disguises to distribute his arrows and messages of love. In this valentine's card of 1875 he is seen dressed in contemporary clothing to make a delivery to the home of a young lady.

specific blossoms can be included for their symbolism. For example a posy for a friend who is going away could include rosemary for remembrance, ivy for friendship, juniper for protection or heartsease for its message 'think of me'.

The medieval custom of exchanging or bestowing a 'grace or favour' is an example of a simple, poignant gift. A gallant knight would wear on his arm a 'favour' from his lady – little more than a length of fabric – to show his affection for her.

The day traditionally observed as being for lovers is Valentine's Day on 14 February, a time when those romantically inclined or hopeful of romance, exchange gifts and cards. Mid-February has been associated with young love since the time of the Greeks and Romans; the Romans held their Lupercalian fertility rites in honour of Juno, the goddess of women and marriage, while the Greek goddess was known as Hera. The Christian Church, however, linked this time with Saint Valentine who was executed in 269 AD for holding weddings for young soldiers against the Emperor Claudius's edict – the Emperor believed marriage would impair their fighting spirit.

Many gifts given now as tokens of love were originally, in pagan times, symbols of fertility. Some, especially those made from grain stalks and flowers, were dedicated to Ceres, the goddess of corn and harvest. At harvest time the last sheaf of hay cut and gathered from the fields was believed to contain the spirit of the harvest. It was elaborately decorated and treated with great care and respect in the hope that the spirit, if well looked after, would bring good crops and an abundant harvest the following year. From the large wheat sheaf evolved the smaller and more intricately woven corn dolly. The dolly was hung over doorways in homes for good luck, but was also exchanged by lovers. Dollies are still made today in rural areas. In Ireland the woven corn ears are called the Harvest Knot, in Scotland they are known as Brooches and in England many designs come under the collective title of Country Favours. In some dollies the grains were left on the corn stalks and the number of grains was believed to indicate the number of children a couple might hope to have.

In sheep-farming areas around Northampton in England a similar token to the corn dolly was made, known as a Wooing or a Clipping Posy. Flowers as well as corn were used in its making and the flowers were usually chosen for their heady scent – cabbage roses, larkspur, honeysuckle, wallflowers and gorse among them. An old country saying goes *'when the gorse is out of bloom, kissing is out of season'*. Another herb called southernwood (also known as lad's love), was said to be a 'powerful courting aid', so no doubt the young shepherds of Northampton gathered it by the bunch. In some regions, honeysuckle is never brought into the family house because 'its rich drowsy scent gives daughters erotic dreams' and in Germany a similar embargo is placed on lime flowers.

LOVE AND MARRIAGE

More practical courtship gifts were often exchanged between couples. Cake moulds, butter prints, spoons and other domestic items made of wood were favoured by the Pennsylvanian Dutch, Swiss and Scandinavians. However, the most widespread symbol of love is the ring; its unbroken circle which symbolizes unity has been used to mark an Engagement since the beginning of the Christian era, although previous to this a piece of gold or silver broken in two halves was sometimes shared by a couple to indicate betrothal. Victorians thought that a bride should wear 'a ring on her finger for true love and a brooch on her breast for purity of heart'.

Engagement rings and wedding rings are both worn on the third finger of the left hand because it was once believed that a vein ran through this finger directly to the heart. Many of the customs surrounding marriage have arisen from the traditional fear that there were evil spirits who, if not guarded against, would steal the bride away. Hence the bride is escorted down the aisle by bridesmaids, who protect her by confusing and disorientating these spirits. A bride's bouquet would also once have contained herbs and flowers deemed to be protective or lucky. The throwing of confetti arises from the Eastern tradition of throwing coloured rice to symbolize fertility; nowadays it signifies hopes for wealth and plenty for the couple.

NEWLY WEDS

The giving and receiving of gifts to a bride and groom is customary in most countries. In parts of England a traditional 'Scramble' may still take place, when the groom throws coins to the local children as he leaves the church with his new wife.

11

MAY DAY MORNING

This May Day painting of 1886 by Harriet M Bennett depicts a romantic Victorian scene of children cavorting among springtime blossom.

In the USA, a Bridal Shower party is held for the bride before her wedding day. In Britain a similar event is known as a Hen Night. As with the bridal party, a Baby Shower is given for a mother and her new baby, when friends and relatives bring gifts and celebrate the birth. In Germany a *Freudemaien*, which translates to Joy Posy is brought to the home of the new mother and child.

Some traditional bridal gifts are echoed in the presents given to celebrate the birth of a child. As a bride would have a 'sixpence in the shoe' as a token of future wealth, so a newly born baby would be presented with a small parcel containing a silver coin and bread so that he would never go hungry, a pinch of salt to ensure that his life would never lack savour, matches to light his way and an egg to represent friendship.

MOTHER'S DAY

The role of a mother has long been revered, with Mother Earth being worshipped in many forms. The origins of Mothering Sunday, known in the USA as Mother's Day and celebrated later in the year, are therefore unclear. It may have very early pagan origins but it is probable that it began with the medieval practice of visiting the cathedral of the diocese or Mother Church on the fourth Sunday in Lent. However, the close proximity of Lady Day, celebrated on 25 March and meant to honour the Mother of God, may have contributed to the tradition. The fourth Sunday in Lent is also acknowledged as the day on which the feeding of the five thousand took place. This could explain why it was a day on which the restrictions of Lent were set aside and a feast prepared.

There is no record of the day as a celebration of motherhood among families until the mid-seventeenth century. At that time, people working in service would be given the day off, to visit their mothers who they may not have seen for many months. The principal purpose of the visit was to take her a present, a bunch of flowers or something good to eat; the most common edible gift being the Simnel cake.

Mothering Sunday declined in popularity towards the end of the nineteenth century, but later underwent a revival partly due to the commercially inspired and

SHROVETIDE PARADE

*Shrovetide was a time for merriment and eating before the start
of Lenten fasting and abstinence. This illustration from 1900
shows a carnival-style shrovetide parade in progress.*

separate occasion of Mother's Day in the USA. Initiated in 1907 by a Miss Anna Jarvis who chose the anniversary of her mother's death, the second Sunday in May, to commemorate Mother's Day, World War Two ensured the occasion's success, when many homesick servicemen sent cards home.

EASTER

After Mothering Sunday, Lent culminates in the annual but movable feast of Easter, the date being set by the position of the planets – 'the first Sunday after the full moon, following the Spring Equinox'. However, if the full moon falls on a Sunday, Easter Day is celebrated the following week. Easter was originally an Anglo-Saxon pagan festival called *Eosturmonath* after Eostre, the goddess of dawn and spring. Easter is observed in most religions, if not in the Christian context, then as the start of spring, and therefore as a time of rebirth and renewal.

In the Jewish religion, Passover is celebrated to commemorate the liberation of the Israelites from Egypt and the Paschal lamb has become the symbol of Christ as the sacrificial lamb in Christian doctrine. Lamb is therefore a traditional food for this time in both religions, as are eggs which represent rebirth and the continuity of life. For the Passover meal, an egg and a lamb-bone are among the foods arranged on a plate to symbolize aspects of the Passover story, which is ceremonially read. The symbolic food also includes salt-water for tears and bitter herbs for suffering.

There are many traditions associated with Easter and particularly with eggs, but some of the most unusual originate from Germany. For example, in the sixteenth century, young couples exchanged eggs at

HALLOWE'EN

All Hallow Even, known as Hallowe'en, was the time when
spirits roamed free. This Victorian postcard shows the witch,
her black cat and a pumpkin-man.

Eastertime as a way of declaring their intent for one another – if only one was given it meant the relationship would soon end, if six were exchanged, then a marriage would take place.

Rabbits or 'bunnies' are symbols frequently associated with Easter but originally it was the hare, as the animal associated with the goddess Eostre, who portrayed spring. In the USA rabbits have taken the place of European hares, and the brightly coloured and decorated eggs given at Easter are traditionally supposed to be laid by the hare or rabbit. Easter is generally celebrated in April or at the end of March and an old saying still describes excessively exuberant people as being 'Mad as a March Hare'.

HALLOWE'EN

As spring is celebrated as a period of rebirth and renewal, so the fading and passing of the year is also marked. Autumn and the arrival of winter is heralded by Hallowe'en celebrations. These days little effort is made to disguise the pagan origins of the event. Children dress-up in frightening masks and carry gruesomely sculpted pumpkin-face lanterns from house to house, knocking on doors, playing pranks and asking for Trick or Treat. This custom is a natural extension of the pagan tradition of Souling, when village youths would dress like 'the risen souls of the dead' and demons which were said to roam the earth and cause mischief at that time.

Anglo-Saxons commemorated their god of war, Thor, at Hallowe'en and baked a spicy Thor cake, now known as ginger parkin or moggy parkin. The ingredients of oats, butter, treacle and spices were earthly offerings to the god. For Celtic people, 31 October was Winter's Eve and marked the beginning of their new year. In Christian times, attempts were

CHRISTMAS DAY

*Feasting is an important part of the Christmas ritual. This
Swedish painting by Carl Larsson (1894), shows the table
laden with special seasonal foods and decorations.*

made to replace the pagan beliefs and customs with the festivals of All Saints (also known as All Hallows) on 1 November and the feast of All Souls' Day on 2 November, when services were held at which prayers were offered for the departed.

CHRISTMAS AND NEW YEAR

The shortest day (21 December in the northern hemisphere) was the time when the Vikings revelled in their *Juul* or Yule festivities for the worship of their god Odin, burning log fires to help the fading sun. English Druids on the other hand, held the festival of *Nolagh*. Ancient Romans used a seven-day period around the mid-winter date for their festival of *Saturnalia* when gifts were exchanged. Wealthy men gave money and clothing to poorer neighbours and in return received garlands, tapers and grains of incense. But their new year celebration of the *Kalends* (first day of the month)

of January was when gifts were exchanged between families, relatives and children. The roles are reversed in France, where presents to the family are exchanged on the December date of Christmas Day, but gifts to friends and others are given at New Year.

In the fourth century Constantine, the Roman emperor, was converted to Christianity and sensibly decided not to ban pagan festivals completely but to make them Christian celebrations instead. In Britain the Christmas festival on 25 December slowly took hold, superseding Druid rites and only suffering a brief interruption in the seventeenth century, when the Puritan parliament of 1644 declared 'heathen' celebration unlawful, saying that on such a holy day there should be general fasting. Troops were deployed to make sure that no lunches were cooked. With the restoration of the monarchy, the law was repealed and Christmas again became a time of feasting.

15

BOXING DAY MORN

*Both Roman and Victorian households gave gifts to the poor
and needy at Christmas. Boxing Day takes its name from the
boxes of gifts distributed to household servants and from the
alms boxes used by the poor to collect money. This picture,*
Fruit from the Christmas tree *was painted by Arthur Hopkins.*

A boar's head was once the traditional centre-piece
for the Christmas lunch but the turkey has now
become the most important part of the main course.
However, in the Provençal region of the south of
France, the traditional feast consists of 13 desserts
which are laid on the family table after Christmas
mass. Dishes include nougat, water-melon and
quince, jams, *fougasse* or *pompe à huile* (a cake-like
brioche made with olive oil), plums and *calissons
d'aix* (almond paste with hazelnuts and pistachios). A
plate of dates must always be included in the feast,
because of the biblical story in which the leaves of a
palm tree hid and protected Mary one night on her
flight into Egypt. Any one of these 13 sweets could be
individually packaged and thereby transformed into a
tempting festive gift.

Royal Christmas gifts can be traced back to Queen
Elizabeth I who, in 1579, received a satin nightgown
and a sea-water green satin petticoat from Sir Francis
Walsingham – lingerie is still a popular gift. The
Queen also received 'aids to toilet' such as tooth picks
and earpicks, made from precious metals and
encrusted with jewels, perhaps equivalent to contemporary cut-crystal scent bottles and silver-backed hair
brushes. Other popular Elizabethan Christmas gifts
included a 'hogshead of claret, a basket of apples, oys-
ters and puddings' and of course the Christmas ham-
per is also frequently given today.

The day after Christmas, Boxing Day, is also Saint
Stephen's Day. It was traditionally the time when the
wealthy would give alms to the poor, putting their donations into alms boxes. In parts of Britain, it was also
once the day on which a variety of small creatures
were hunted, most commonly the wren. Donations
were then collected on its behalf – a custom which has
fortunately ceased.

In parts of the world, New Year is still celebrated
more widely than Christmas – in Scotland, Hogmanay
is the more important of the two festivals. Part of the
New Year ritual in the north of England as well as Scotland, includes First Footing. A tall, dark stranger (the
first footer) should knock on the front door of a home at
midnight and be the first person to cross the threshold
in the new year. He is admitted carrying a gift of

coal to be placed on the fire. This is supposed to ensure that the hearth of the home will never go cold during the coming year, and to bring health and good fortune to the family. The French *Noël* and Italian *Natale* originally celebrated the birth of the new year, but have been adopted to commemorate Christ's birth.

Twelfth Night on 5 January, is now most commonly observed as the night that heralds the end of Christmas, when decorations are taken down. In pagan times it was the time for wassailing, when to *Wes heill* meant to be whole, healthy and free of evil spirits, but it has now been absorbed into the Christian celebration of Epiphany on 6 January. Gangs of youths would bang drums and clash cymbals in orchards and fields, to frighten evil spirits away. To quench the revellers' thirst after all this activity they drank a traditional Wassailing Cup, made from warm brown ale, sherry, spices, roasted apples and lemons, or a similar concoction called Lamb's Wool.

A custom once popular in England but now only observed in France is the Twelfth Night Cake or *Galette des Rois* which is baked with a bean hidden in it. Whoever gets the slice of cake with the bean becomes the king and, with a chosen partner, rules over the festivities for the rest of the day. In Italy, 5 January is known as *La Befana*, when children put out their stockings, expecting an old witch-like woman (who represents the dying year) to pass by, leaving gifts.

Ephiphany is acknowledged as the time when the Three Wise Men brought their offerings of gold, frankincense and myrrh to the infant Christ in the stable. It is probably from this event that the Christmas tradition of gift-giving derives. The original gifts had prophetic meanings: gold for the King, frankincense to anoint and embalm His wounds, and bitter myrrh to represent the pain He would later experience.

Traditional Gifts aims to revive interest in home-made gifts. The unique collection of specially selected gifts, some with ancient origins and others from more recent sources, offers a wide variety of choice, suitable for most occasions and capabilities. They have been created by contemporary craftspeople who value quality and authenticity, some being amongst the last still working in their particular field.

THE WASSAIL BOWL

This nineteenth-century illustration shows a Wassail Bowl filled with warm, spicy ale being taken to revellers who have paraded round the village homes and farms frightening away the old year's bad spirits.

BIRTHDAYS AND SPECIAL OCCASIONS

For almost all of us, a birthday or special celebration is a time when we are given indulgent gifts; things we would not normally buy ourselves, such as special garments, luxurious scented bath lotions or mouth-watering and delicious edible delights.

When the Raj ruled India, birthdays were very often celebrated with a grand weigh-in. The Maharaja would sit in a dish-like seat on one side of a pair of giant golden weighing scales. Faithful subjects, family-members and allies would fill the opposite side of the scales with gifts of gold and jewels until the Maharaja's weight had been more than equalled and he would rise gradually into the air alongside his gifts.

GIVE US THE LUXURIES OF LIFE, AND WE WILL
DISPENSE WITH ITS NECESSITIES.

John Lothrop Motley

HERBS AND THEIR USES

FENNEL

Fennel is generally grown as an annual although in warm climates it is a perennial. The white bulb of the Florence variety can be grated raw into salads, or blanched and baked as a vegetable, while the leaves and seeds of common fennel are useful for their liquorice taste, adding a fresh flavour to fish and cheese. An infusion of fennel leaves is held to be a soothing lotion for bathing tired eyes and a toning skin tonic.

GARLIC

Garlic is a popular plant in the kitchen for the use of its root, and although synonymous with French cookery, it is also widely used in Italian and Indian dishes, its pungent flavour and odour mellowing with cooking. Well-known for its antiseptic and medicinal properties, garlic is used as a cure for a variety of ailments including indigestion, rheumatism and colds. Garlic was traditionally used as a deterrent to ward-off vampires and evil spirits.

SAGE

Sage has long been respected for its medicinal properties. Nicholas Culpeper, the renowned seventeenth-century British herbalist, recommended 'gargles likewise made with Sage.... with some honey put thereto to wash sore Mouthes and Throats'. Well-respected cooks added sage and onion to stuffings for fatty meats such as goose and pork. In consideration of both its medicinal and culinary uses, sage signifies domestic virtue.

MARJORAM

Marjoram has a strong, savoury flavour which precludes it from being used in cosmetic recipes, but makes it ideal for use in cookery. Sprigs of marjoram are often added to dishes containing tomatoes, chicken, game and beef, and to sausages to give a herbal flavour. Marjoram is another herb that thrives in sunlight. There is an old saying that 'golden Marjoram will remain green with jealousy unless it is allowed a proper share of the sun'.

PARSLEY

Parsley is a commonly used herb and is regarded as the staple plant of any herb garden. Although difficult to grow it is said in folklore to thrive in the house where 'the mistress is the master'. It also grows well when planted in the shade of a rose bush. Chewing a few parsley leaves is said to quench the lingering smell of garlic on the breath, and an infusion of the plant was often taken as a tonic, and as a relief for rheumatic pains.

ROSEMARY

Rosemary, also known as Dew of the Sea because of its preference for sunny coastal areas, is an evergreen which, in early May, produces tiny violet-blue flowers that are attractive to bees. The fragrant rosemary plant provides an almost constant supply of the culinary herb, frequently used with roast meats, in stuffings and as a flavouring for vinegar. Rosemary is an emblem of remembrance but can be given as a love token.

MINT

Mint has many varieties such as peppermint, spearmint, apple mint and Scotch mint. It is an easy plant to grow but can be invasive so it is best to plant mint in a tub or pot. Although most frequently made into jelly or sauce and used as an accompaniment to roast lamb, sprigs of mint are also placed on top of new potatoes and peas. In medicinal recipes, it is used in footbaths, moth bags and as an aid to digestion. Mint is the plant that represents virtue.

THYME

Thyme grows best in a sunny area of the garden. The plant, whose varieties include lemon, caraway and Silver Queen, will not lose its leaves in winter, so provides a constant fresh herb supply for the kitchen; it can also be dried successfully. Thyme is used in many stews and sauces and is often added to chicken and egg dishes as well as to meat-based pies. Thyme is a symbol of activity.

EDIBLE SPICE WREATH

FILLING THE WREATH FRAME

Fit a firmly packed layer of dried moss between the support rings and tie firmly. This makes the base onto which decorations can be fixed.

ATTACHING THE DECORATIONS

When the frame is covered and secure, attach a variety of attractive and useful spices using small loops of wire, decorative braids or ribbons.

TO FORM THE BASIC FRAME, MAKE two rings of sturdy metal (you could use coathangers depending on the size of wreath you wish to make). Use a smaller ring to form the inner edge of the wreath and a slightly larger one for the outer rim. Fix a number of small wedges of wood, cardboard or folded wire between the two rings to keep them an equal distance apart all the way around. Fill the space between the two rings with closely packed moss and bind securely in place with fine string or raffia. Alternatively you could use florists' foam held in place with fine mesh wire. Cover over and disguise the bindings and any untidy end pieces by carefully tucking extra moss around them.

With short lengths of fine florists' wire bent into loops, or hair pins (not clips or kirby grips), arrange and fix a selection of spices and aromatic flowers to the metal base. Small oranges covered with cloves tucked into the rind give off a sweet and spicy aroma and can be used for flavouring in mulled wine or baked ham; while daintily grouped bunches of cinnamon bark or vanilla pods create good contrasts; nutmeg, mace, star annis and ginger lightly covered with a dusting of gold leaf add variety of texture and colour.

To make the herbal wreath on page 21, tie bunches of dried and fresh herbs to the ring, instead of spices. Attach miniature terracotta plant pots to the base of the wreath by tying raffia tightly under the lip of the pot and using the end-lengths of raffia to tie the pots securely to the wreath-frame. Fill the pots with small sachets of home-made bouquet garni, cloves of garlic, sweet-smelling lavender or rosemary, or even dried chillies.

For a more decorative wreath, try adding loops of hessian rope and pieces of calico or sacking amongst the bunches of herbs and spices. Festive wreaths can be made more colourful by intertwining ribbons and glittering braids in between the rings. Bunches of dried hops or small cobs of maize, and flowers such as the daisy-like camomile can be used to play up a seasonal theme.

SPICE OF LIFE

The finished ring is not only visually pleasing, but the spices will provide a keen cook with a handy supply of ingredients.

EDIBLE GIFTS

NATURALLY-FLAVOURED VINEGARS and oils, savoury pickles, relishes and sweet preserves have long been given as gifts. Family recipes were often fiercely guarded and passed on through generations. As certain ingredients were sometimes hard to come by, only one family in a village may have grown a particular fruit or vegetable, so the jar of pickle or preserve made from the crop and given as a gift, would have been not only a treat but a special sign of friendship. In Austria, a Christmas custom still practised today, is for women to make and give *petit fours* as presents. Each home has its own particular biscuit-cutter whose shape is prided as being unique.

These days, delicately-flavoured herb vinegars are often used alone, as a dressing, or made into mayonnaise or savoury sauces. Traditionally, vinegar was also used as a cure for a sore throat, being credited with disinfectant properties. It was also sometimes worn as a scent or perfume. Women would carry small vials or bottles of aromatic vinegar on chains around their necks or waists, to revive them should they feel faint, or as a remedy for a headache.

In flavoured oils, the curative properties of the herbs are released and the more herb in proportion to oil, the stronger and more effective the mixture is.

NATURAL FLAVOURINGS

The infusion of fragrant herbs and spices gives a piquant flavour to plain oils and vinegars; when beautifully presented in labelled bottles, they make perfect gifts.

GILLIFLOWER JELLY

Makes approximately 900ml (1½pts)

25g (1oz) gilliflower (Dianthus caryophyllus) petals, freshly picked
500g (1¼lbs) sugar
500ml (16fl oz) water
250ml (8fl oz) liquid pectin

Liquidize the petals and infuse in hot (not boiling) water for a few minutes (but no longer than 15 minutes). Strain and retain water and petals separately. Boil together the liquid and sugar then stir in the pectin. Bring to the boil again and, after a minute, remove any foam. Add the gilliflower petals, stir thoroughly, then remove the liquid from the heat. Let it stand for about five minutes before spooning into a jar. Use plain glass jam jars and apply decorative labels to each one.

GILLIFLOWER JELLY

Gilliflower (Dianthus Caryophyllus), made by infusing the flower petals.

TOMATO RELISH

Makes approximately 2kg (3½lbs)

375g (13oz) chopped onions
225ml (8fl oz) malt vinegar
1kg (2lb 3oz) tomatoes, chopped
1 teaspoon pickling mustard
15g (½oz) salt
1 teaspoon ground black pepper
250g (9oz) raw cane sugar

Put the onions and the vinegar into a pan and heat until the onions have softened. Add the tomatoes, mustard, salt and pepper, then bring the mixture to the boil. Add the sugar and simmer until the consistency is thick and not too runny. Allow to cool a little then put in tightly sealed warm jars and use as a tasty accompaniment to cheese, cold meat and salads.

DILL DRESSING
Makes 200ml (7fl oz)

40g (1½oz) mild American mustard
20g (¾oz) sugar
30ml (1fl oz) white wine vinegar
90ml (3fl oz) good quality vegetable oil
1 teaspoon fresh dill, chopped
A pinch of salt
A pinch of freshly ground black pepper

Place all the ingredients in a bowl and mix thoroughly. Put in a bottle with a tight lid and use with fish and cheese dishes.

APPLE AND WALNUT HORSERADISH

Makes 450g (1lb)

150g (5oz) grated horseradish
50g (2oz) grated apple
50g (2oz) skinned and chopped walnuts
1 tablespoon lemon juice
1 tablespoon wine vinegar or sherry
1 teaspoon sugar (optional)
140ml (¼pt) double cream (add at a later date if not for immediate use)

Place all the ingredients in a bowl and mix thoroughly. Only add the cream if the sauce is intended for immediate use, otherwise add it just before eating. If the consistency is too thick add a little more cream. Allow to stand in a cool place for half an hour before serving.

MUSTARD WITH BEER
Makes 2-3 small mustard pots

60g (3oz) crushed black and white mustard seeds
A large pinch of sea or rock salt
2-3 tablespoons malt vinegar
2-3 tablespoons beer

Place all the ingredients in a bowl and mix well together. Pot in lidded jars. Eat with cold meat and sausages or use as an ingredient for sauces.

APPLE AND WALNUT HORSERADISH

The English people's love of roast beef earned them the nickname 'Les Rosbifs'. Horseradish sauce accompanies this dish.

COURGETTE AND TOMATO CHUTNEY

Makes 1.8kg (4lbs)

1.25kg (2lbs) courgettes, chopped or sliced
375g (13oz) tomatoes, chopped or sliced
375g (13oz) onions, chopped or sliced
250g (9oz) sultanas
125g (4oz) salt
500ml (1pt) malt vinegar
1 teaspoon ground cinnamon
500g (1lb 2oz) sugar

Place all the ingredients except the sugar into a preserving pan that is not made from copper and cook slowly for about half an hour. Add the sugar and continue to cook until the consistency is thick and not runny. Allow to cool a little and then put into warm jars and cover tightly.

TOMATO RELISH

In Britain a traditional country meal, known as a 'Ploughman's lunch' consisted of a piece of bread with cheese and pickle. This spicy tomato relish is typical of the pickle eaten with the lunch.

HERB OIL

Take some good quality sunflower oil, olive oil or groundnut oil and an assortment of perfectly fresh herbs. Wash the herbs thoroughly and shake well to dry. Put them in a bottle and pour in the oil. Leave for 10 to 14 days to allow the flavour of the herbs to permeate the oil. The oil can then be used to add extra flavouring to most dishes.

ROSEMARY FLOWER VINEGAR

Take some good quality white wine vinegar and add a large sprig of fresh rosemary which has as many flowers open as possible. Leave for at least 24 hours – the longer the rosemary remains in the vinegar, the stronger the flavour will be. This vinegar is an ideal way of adding a subtle rosemary flavour to lamb marinades, salad dressings and casseroles.

LEMON VINEGAR

Wash a fresh lemon and peel as long a strip of zest as possible from it. Add to good quality white wine vinegar then allow the zest to flavour the vinegar for at least 24 hours. The longer it is left, the stronger the flavour will be. The vinegar can be used to give a fresh and sharp taste to salad dressings and mayonnaise as well as fish sauces.

NARROW-BOAT WARE

THE MEN AND WOMEN WHO SAILED narrow boats along the waterways of England created a unique style of painted enamelware, said to be the oldest folk-art in the country. Today only a handful of narrow-boat painters are still at work, yet a novice can apply a simplified version of the classic narrow-boat designs to dull household items, and transform them with the colours and vitality of the original ware. Canal traditions are also popular in France as well as Holland where distinctive styles of decoration have evolved over the centuries.

During the Industrial Revolution in the seventeenth century, the transportation of raw materials and finished goods switched from roads to waterways because it was quicker and cheaper. Where rivers did not exist, cuts were made into the land and then flooded to link one stretch of water to another; these cuts and canals formed a network across the country. At first boatmen worked and travelled alone, sleeping in a tent or on the river bank. As the canal system developed, they journeyed further away and were parted from their wives and families for weeks at a time. To end these separations, small cabins were built on the stern or back of the boats to give boatmen a permanent

CANAL CLASSICS

Traditionally pots and pans were transformed by the art of skilled narrow-boat painters. The paint itself protected the metal items from rust and wear.

28

29

BUCKETS AND BOWLS

*Far off castles and river-bank flowers provided inspiration for
painters of narrow-boat enamelware. Although their choice of
paint colours was limited, their talent was considerable.*

place to rest and to accommodate their families. The cabins were small – space meant money to the boatman – so furnishings were kept to a minimum and what little there was doubled up; tables became beds and doors folded up to provide seats. The few possessions kept on board were painted to make them more homely and appealing, while the exterior of the cabin was painted not only to make it look distinctive and attractive, but to weatherproof and protect the wood as well.

From this naïve painting evolved the traditional designs we see today. The colours are believed to have been mainly primary because, being the cheaper shades of paint, these are the ones which would have been readily available on board. Painting techniques became more refined over the years, but the original symbols and stories were still evident.

Traditional narrow-boat painting was applied to three basic utensils: the Buckby can – a covered watering can for holding the supply of drinking water; a hand bowl – a round basin with handle for scooping water from the canals to use in washing and cleaning; and a Nosh bowl – a large dish from which the horse pulling the narrow boat ate his oats. The bases rather than the insides of the bowls were painted because they were stored upside down on the deck, so it was the base that the boatman looked on as he steered his boat through the canals.

Cabin paintings were often framed by panels belonging to the boat's structure, painted in bright yellow. Inside these frames were depicted turreted castles flying pennant flags and surrounded by snow-capped mountains and bright blue skies. A lake with a boat on it and a man crossing a hump-backed bridge would have often appeared in the foreground. The castles seen on many old narrow boats are said to resemble the grand old buildings in the Carpathian Mountains of Eastern Europe.

To this day, on the bow of a narrow boat, a stylized eye symbol is usually present. This can be traced back through centuries and is popular on fishing boats in countries such as Greece and Portugal. Its origin relates to the belief that a boat has a soul and the soul must be able to see where it is going, so an eye is painted on either side of the bow to give a clear view of the way ahead.

Roses are a very popular feature of enamelware, drawing their inspiration from the banks and hedgerows along the towpath. Each documented narrow-boat painter has his own style of rose, and experts can tell who painted a particular piece by examining the flowers.

Green, red, yellow and blue are the main colours used for decorating, although brown is occasionally included. The painting technique used is similar to fabric printing in that colour is built up layer by layer. Each layer is left to dry and then varnished before the next one is applied; this results in an almost three-dimensional effect. The first layer is a solid colour painted all over the tin object. Then, where the design is to be applied, a background colour is added. Detail colours such as the green for leaves and base flower shades are filled in next and finally, the detail colour for flower stamens and leaf veins is painted. With modern durable enamel paint it is not strictly necessary to varnish between each application, but one coat over the finished paintwork will give added protection.

If you want to use traditional narrow-boat motifs to decorate smaller items such as tea mugs and milk jugs, they can be bought already enamelled in a single plain

BASIC BEGINNINGS

Dull, plain galvanized metal buckets and pans await the artist's brush. Connoisseurs are able to recognize the work of individual narrow-boat painters as well as identify which specific canal the work originates from.

THERE IS NOTHING –
ABSOLUTELY NOTHING –
HALF SO MUCH WORTH DOING
AS SIMPLY MESSING ABOUT IN
BOATS

*The Wind in the Willows, Chapter One,
Kenneth Grahame*

colour onto which you can paint your own designs. Larger items such as buckets, coal scuttles and watering cans are generally bought in their plain grey galvanized state. These need to be prepared with a couple of coats of base colour before more detailed decoration can be applied on the top.

Although traditional narrow-boat tinware was painted with roses and other fauna and flora found in the hedgerows along the towpaths, inspiration for your own enamelware designs might be found by looking at other decorative details from the boats themselves. For example, intricately knotted and plaited ropes were nailed to the 'Ram's head' or rudder of the 'butty' or boat, and thick rope fenders were used to protect the bow of the boat from knocking against the river bank. Twisted and plaited rope patterns could provide interesting borders, as could rows of tiny diamond shapes painted in alternating colours – diamonds were very popular as a theme in narrow-boat painting, as were three-leaved shamrocks. Designs may also incorporate fine lace-like patterns to reflect the delicate lace-rim plates that were both popular with and avidly collected by the women who lived on the boats. The plates were usually displayed on the walls inside the cabin, providing homely decoration in the small, cramped living area.

To personalize your enamelware gift, it is quite in keeping with traditional themes to apply names, initials or monograms. On many of the old narrow boats the vessel's name was painted on the bow and sides of the cabin. In sympathy with the authentic style, letters should be shaded with an additional line of darker paint to make them stand out against the coloured background of the design.

GUERNSEY JUMPERS

KNITTED GARMENTS FROM the Channel Island of Guernsey, situated between the south coast of England and the north of France, have been popular gifts since the reign of Queen Elizabeth I. The fine quality stockings knitted on the island at that time were often given to the royalty.

The style of tubular knitting which was used to make a Guernsey jumper was developed from the traditional method of knitting stockings – in the round, on four needles. However, instead of using four needles as you would for socks or stockings, as many as eleven needles may be used for a jumper.

The close-fitting *Corset de Poissonier*, as the fisherman's jumper is called locally in the old French patois or dialect, is made from three knitted tubes, a large one forming the body and two smaller ones for the arms. Originally holes were cut into the body tube for the sleeves to be set-in and joined.

For the *Corset de Poissonier*, the basic pattern is simple, using only garter or knit and purl stitches. Different designs are made by varying the repeat or sequence of these stitches, but only in units of one to ten – low numbers were easy to remember and could be counted on fingers. The patterns had to be simple and easily memorized because women knitted while they worked.

SEAFARER'S SWEATER

Fisherman Bill Harvey, photographed mending Lobster pots in Porthgwarra in 1903, wears a traditional fisherman's jumper in the Channel-Islands style.

Traditional Guernsey jumpers were simply but distinctively patterned using symbols associated with the family and home of the wearer. For example, a fisherman who lived in the parish of Forest may have had a triangular zig-zag motif, representing trees, around the arm of his jumper. The patterns for these designs were never written down, but passed on by word-of-mouth from mother to daughter, and many have been lost over the years. The motifs in the jumper were not purely decorative, but were also used as a way of identifying the owner should he have been washed overboard and drowned. The knitted symbols were deciphered to determine from which family and what parish the man had come. The *chef de famille* or head of the family would not usually wear the same pattern as younger family members or workers, but the relevant symbols would be incorporated in his Guernsey.

There are stories that say the basic patterns on the Guernsey jumper represent the island and its way of life. For example, the knotted edge where the jumper is cast on, is seen as evocative of the pebbles on the shore line, while the wavy stitch patterns on the welt of the jumper are said to symbolize the sea surrounding the island. Above the welt, a box-shaped motif is said to look like the cork floats of the fishermen's nets and around the arm and shoulder are chain-stitch seams which look like ship's ropes.

The wool traditionally used to knit a Guernsey is natural, still retaining the lanolin which makes it waterproof. The recognizable blue colour is achieved using European woad, which will dye through the oily base of the wool. Guernsey jumpers are made on the island today, although most are now knitted by machines and hand finished.

INSTRUCTIONS FOR KNITTING A GUERNSEY JUMPER

This pattern is based on the instruction leaflet of an old Guernsey firm which is no longer in business. It is said to take approximately 80 hours to knit a Guernsey in the traditional manner.

MATERIALS

5-ply worsted wool for 91cm (36in) chest, 750g (26oz); for 102cm (40in) chest, 900g (32oz); for 112cm (44in) chest, 1050g (37oz).
4-ply worsted wool for 61cm (24in) chest, 250g (9oz); for 71cm (28in) chest, 400g (14oz); for 81cm (32in) chest, 500g (7oz); for 91cm (36in) chest, 650g (23oz). Yarn amounts are approximate.
For 5-ply Guernsey: One 2¼mm (size 13) circular needle, 76cm (30in) long
For 4-ply Guernsey: One 2¼mm (size 13) circular needle, 61cm (24in) long.
Pair of long 2¼mm (size 13) needles.
Set of four long 2¼mm (size 13) double-pointed needles. If desired the whole garment may be made using eleven 2¼mm (size 13) double-pointed needles, varying the number of needles according to the number of stitches being worked.

TENSION

32 sts to 10cm (4in) in width over stocking stitch using 5-ply.
34 sts to 10cm (4in) in width over stocking stitch using 4-ply.
As tension varies with knitters, measurements should be carefully checked.

MEASUREMENTS

Actual chest measurements: 95,105,117 (65,75,86,95)cm [37½, 41½, 46 (25½, 29½, 34, 37½) in]

ABBREVIATIONS

k – knit; p – purl; st(s) – stitches(es); in(s) – inch(es); cm(s) – centimetre(s); tog – together; cont – continue; g st – garter stitch, k on every row; st st – stocking stitch, k every round when working in rounds, k on right side and p on wrong side work working in rows.
NOTE: If preferred, the knotted edge method of casting on may be used.

KNOTTED CASTING ON

Using the thumb method and a single strand of yarn, *cast 2 sts on to right-hand needle, with tip of left-hand needle cast off the first of these 2 sts; repeat from * until you have the required number of sts.
Instructions written for 5-ply sizes – 91cm (36in), 102cm (40in) and 112cm (44in) chests. 4-ply sizes in brackets – 61cm (24in), 71cm (28in), 81cm (32in) and 91cm (36in) chests.

BODY

Garter st edging Cast on 140,156,174 (98,116,134,150) sts for back on a long 2¼mm (size 13) needle. Cont in garter st and k 24,24,24(16,16,20,24) rows. Leave work aside and knit another piece exactly the same for front. Using circular needle join both pieces as follows. K across sts of front then on to same needle k across sts of back. 280, 312, 348(196,232,268,300) sts. Cont in rounds. Work 8,8,8(6,6,6,6) rounds in k2, p2 rib. From this point the garment is knitted almost entirely in st st, with a single purl st at each side edge – called the 'seam st'. For this follow up the last st from garter st edging and cont to purl them throughout.
Next round all k, increasing 20 sts evenly across round. 300, 332, 368 (216, 252, 288, 320) sts. Cont straight in st st with purl seam stitches until required length

allowing approximately 24, 26, 27(18, 19, 20, 22)cm [9½,10,10½(7, 7½,8, 8½)in] for armholes.
At this point the knitting may be continued right up to the shoulder, and after casting off the armholes are cut and rolled and the sleeves inserted. This may seem unusual but it is the traditional way. ARMHOLE A.
Alternatively, the armholes may be worked by dividing the sts for back and front, then cont knitting the two pieces separately on the long 2¼mm (size 13) needles up to the shoulders. After casting off, the sleeves are inserted in the usual way. ARMHOLE B.

ARMHOLE A

Next round Cast on 6 sts over each seam st – the centre of these 7 sts becomes the new seam st. Complete the round ending with the second seam st and rearranging the last few sts so that the last st on the round is the new second seam st.
1st round K6, p6, k to 12 sts before first seam st, p6, k6, p seam st, k6, p6, k to last 13 sts of round, p6, k6, p seam st.
2nd round K all sts except seam stitches which are purled. Repeat these 2 rounds until you have the required depth to form the armholes.

ARMHOLE B

Divide sts for front and back, the seam sts are now discontinued.
Front Use long 2¼mm (size 13) needles.
1st row k4, p6, k to last 10 sts, p6, k4.Row 2 All p. Repeat these 2 rows until you have the required depth for armholes ending with wrong side row.
Back Work exactly as front.
Now continue both ARMHOLE A and ARMHOLE B as follows.
Divide sts for shoulders allowing

KNIT ONE PURL ONE

It is said to take approximately 80 hours to knit a Guernsey sweater, although only simple knit and purl stitches are used.

46,50,54(30,36,42,46) sts for each shoulder – remember to allow an extra 3 sts for each shoulder if ARMHOLE A has been worked. The centre 58,66,76(48,54, 60,68) sts at front and back are for neck.

SHOULDER

With wrong sides facing, join shoulder by casting off together one st from front and one st from back, finishing with the 47th,51st,55th(31st,37th,43rd,47th) st left on needle at neck edge.

NECK GUSSET

With this last st start neck gusset by knitting one st from front and one st from back alternately (working one row k and one row p alternately) until you have 19,19,19(13,15,17,17) sts on left-hand needle which forms the gusset and have worked 18,18,18(12,14,16,16) rows. K across these sts then k to other shoulder. Cast off second shoulder, as before, until you are left with the 47th or appropriate stitch on needle. Work second gusset as first gusset. 114,130,150(94,106,118, 134) sts. Increasing 2 sts on first round work 5cm (2in) in k2, p2 rib. Cast off in rib.

SLEEVES

Using 4 needles cast on 72,80,84 (48, 52,60,76) sts.

Work in rounds of k2, p2 rib for 10,10, 10(8,8,8,8)cm[4,4,4(3,3,3,3)in]. Change to st st. Inc 6 sts evenly across first round and one st at end of round for the 'seam' st. 79,87,91(55,59,67,83) sts. Work 6 rounds in st st keeping seam st.

Next round Inc in first st, k to last 2 sts, inc in next st, p seam st. Cont increasing in this way on every 6th round until there are 109,121,129 (81,87,99,117) sts. Cont straight without further shaping until sleeve is required length allowing approximately 6,6,6 (4,4,5,6)cm [$2^{1}/_{2}$,$2^{1}/_{2}$,$2^{1}/_{2}$ ($1^{1}/_{2}$,$1^{1}/_{2}$,2,$2^{1}/_{2}$) in] for gusset (i.e. if 51cm (20in) sleeve is required for adult's size make sleeve 44cm ($17^{1}/_{2}$in) before starting gusset.)

SLEEVE GUSSET

1st round Increase in first st, k to last 3 sts, increase in next st, k1 p seam st.
Round 2 and all alternate rounds. Work straight.
3rd round Increase in second st, k to last 4 sts, increase in next st, k2, p seam st. Cont in this way widening the gusset by increasing on alternate rounds until 12,12,14 (7,8,10,12) increase rounds have been worked. Continue straight working the gusset stitches in st st and the remaining sts in k2, p2 rib for 8,8,8(6,6,6,6) rounds. Cast off the ribbed sts on next round but cont working the gusset in rows of st st, decreasing 1 st at each end of every k row until 3 sts remain. P3 tog and fasten off.

TO COMPLETE ARMHOLE A

Cut along seam st on armholes, roll edge in and hem. Sew top of sleeve and gusset around hem of armhole.

ARMHOLE B

Sew top of sleeve and gusset into armhole.

CHILDREN

GIFTS FOR CHILDREN ARE OFTEN THE most pleasurable to give. A child's uninhibited curiosity and delight are more than enough reward for the time and effort taken in the gift's making.

Amongst the most enduring and endearing toys are the simple, soft rag doll and animals such as the floppy-eared rabbit or bow-tied teddy bear. Many of these soft toys survive the rigors of childhood 'affection', lasting in to their owner's adult years. Their naïve charm still has appeal in contemporary playrooms among numerous metal space-ships and moulded plastic games.

WHEN I AM GROWN TO MAN'S ESTATE
I SHALL BE VERY PROUD AND GREAT,
AND TELL THE OTHER GIRLS AND
BOYS NOT TO MEDDLE WITH MY TOYS.

Looking Forward, Robert Louis Stevenson

NEW ARRIVALS

THE ARRIVAL OF A NEW BABY has long been surrounded with traditions and customs. The day, date and time of the birth is said to influence the child's future. Western cultures look to the zodiac signs for glimpses of what is to come, and in the Orient, Chinese horoscopes with animal symbols, including the cat, tiger, buffalo and monkey, are used. Each person is said to display the same characteristics of the particular animal in whose horoscope year they were born.

Many birth and birthday traditions have pagan origins and are precautions to guard newborn infants against evil and illness. Gifts of clothing and bed-linen are common; originally it was believed that the first thing a new-born baby should be wrapped in was a worn cloth, so the father's shirt or mother's petticoat was often used to swaddle the new arrival.

Jewellery, especially the amulet in Egyptian and Roman times, was thought to be an effective way to carry the charm and protection offered by silver because it was worn close to the skin. However, this could also explain the popularity of spoons, bowls, napkin rings and tankards made from silver. Gifts to mark a baby's birth may have originated in the presents which the Three Wise Men gave to the Christ child.

'EVERY BABY BORN INTO THE WORLD IS FINER THAN THE LAST.'

Nicholas Nickleby, Charles Dickens

BIRTHSTONES

Birth gem stones are often given in the form of jewellery to a newly born or young child, and may be chosen again later in life as the stone for an engagement ring. Healing properties and powers have long been attributed to gem stones: the Ancient Egyptians believed turquoise guarded against illness, while the Romans wore natal gems as talismans or charms. Birthstones are paired with the zodiac signs, so there are often two associated with one month, for example the first half of July which comes under the sign of Cancer is linked to the ruby, whereas Leo, encompassing the latter half of July and early August, takes the cornelian as its stone.

The garnet, a symbol of constancy and fidelity, is the stone for January; amethyst which protects against violent passions is known as February's gem. Early March takes the aquamarine and later March the bloodstone, sign of wisdom and steadfast affection. The first half of April is associated with the rock crystal; the latter part of the month with the diamond, the stone of innocence and purity. May is divided between emeralds and chrysoprase and June takes the pearl, the symbol of wealth, as its gem, as well as the moonstone. August's gems are peridot and sardonyx, while sapphires and lapis lazuli are for September. The opal of early October is said to be unlucky to those not born to wear it, while the end of October has the tourmaline as its gem. The year ends with topaz for those born in November, and turquoise and zircon for December.

Coral was once a popular gift for newborn babies as it was said to have the power to ease the pain of teething. A midwife would also often hang a necklace woven from nine strands of scarlet silk around a baby's neck, as a charm to soothe teething pains.

BABY'S BLANKET

*A cot quilt is a useful and decorative gift, and one that may be
passed down through the generations of a family.*

MONDAY'S CHILD IS FAIR OF FACE,
TUESDAY'S CHILD IS FULL OF GRACE,
WEDNESDAY'S CHILD IS FULL OF WOE,
THURSDAY'S CHILD HAS FAR TO GO,
FRIDAY'S CHILD IS LOVING AND GIVING,
SATURDAY'S CHILD WORKS HARD FOR
ITS LIVING,
AND THE CHILD THAT IS BORN ON
THE SABBATH DAY
IS BONNY, BLITHE AND GOOD AND GAY.

BABIES' CLOTHES

BABY'S BONNET

*Babies' heads need to be protected from the cold, so a bonnet is
an ideal gift for a new arrival. Any parent would be proud of a
specially created, coordinated outfit of bonnet and bootees.*

BABY GOWN

MATERIALS

2m (2¹/₂yds) fine white cotton
White cotton thread, pins, needles
Lace tape, if desired
Narrow satin ribbon for back ties
*Broad satin ribbon for neckline facing, if
desired*

Cut the following pattern pieces
1 skirt length
1 bodice piece
2 sleeves

Neatly hem the cuff edge of the sleeve.
Turn the cut sleeve piece inside out and
fold in half, right sides together. Stitch
along the open side, 6mm (¹/₄in) from the
edge, to form the sleeve. Repeat to make
the second sleeve. Sew a single even row of
running stitch around the top of the sleeve
and gather slightly so that the sleeve becomes the same size as the sleeve opening
in the bodice.

Turn the bodice piece inside out so right
sides are together. Hem the edges of the
back opening and around the neck. An additional interfacing or binding of broad
satin ribbon can be added around the
neckline on the wrong side to give additional quality to the finish.

Stitch neatly along the shoulders, leaving a 6mm (¹/₄in) seam allowance. Place
the sleeve in the sleeve hole. Gradually pin
or tack the sleeve in place, so that the
sleeve seam is on the underside and the
armhole seam and excess fabric are on the
wrong side. Repeat for the other sleeve
then sew into place with neat, close
stitches to finish off.

Hem along the bottom edge of the skirt length and both sides. Make two rows of fine running stitch along the top edge of the skirt. Gather the material along the threads, concentrating the bulk of the fabric in the centre. Lay the fabric wrong side down and fold the two edges into the centre, right sides facing. Place the bodice on top and gently ease and gather the fabric to a corresponding size, again ensuring that the bulk of the fabric lies in the middle front, and that the fabric is almost flat from the centre back to under the arms. Sew securely in place, keeping the seam to the wrong side of the dress. Turn the whole garment the right way round and iron.

RIBBON TIES

Cut six pairs (12 pieces) of narrow satin ribbon lengths 10cm (4in) long, to make ties to hold the sides of the dress together. Sew one of the pair of ties on either side of the top of the bodice at the neck, keeping the stitchwork on the wrong side. Repeat at the base of the bodice and at regular intervals along the back of the skirt, until all are in place.

FIRST FINERY

A baby's first white gown with matching bonnet and bootees is traditionally adorned with silk embroidery and trimmed with fine lace. In biblical times new-born babies were 'swaddled' in cloth strips, and during the Victorian era both boys and girls wore dresses, so this charming ensemble, usually worn for a baptism, is suitable for a baby of either sex.

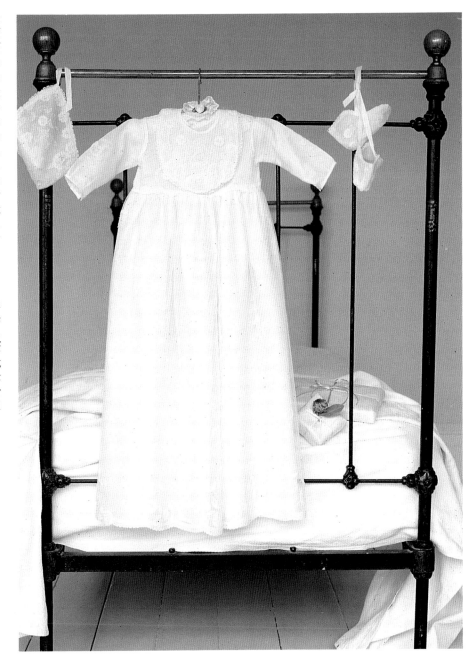

FIRST STEPS

*Much sentiment is attached to a baby's first pair
of shoes. These bootees are easy to create and
would make a delightful keepsake for a nostalgic
mother to pass to the next generation.*

BOOTEES

Cut two of each pattern piece

TOE AREA
Neatly hem from point I to corresponding point I on piece D. Place the main boot piece wrong side down. Place piece A on top of point A on the base piece, so the centres of both pieces are lined up. Gather the edge of point A to fit around point D to mark II on either side of D. Gather slightly to help fit and pin in place. When D fits neatly into point A, secure by sewing.

INFANT JOY

'I HAVE NO NAME;
I AM BUT TWO DAYS OLD.'
WHAT SHALL I CALL THEE?
'I HAPPY AM,
JOY IS MY NAME.'
SWEET JOY BEFALL THEE!

William Blake

HEEL
Keeping the fabric wrong way round, stitch a neat seam to join together the two pieces of heel fabric. Fold up heel flap E into place and sew. Turn the whole bootee right way round and sew a 10cm (4in) length of satin ribbon on either side of the front of the bootee so that it can be tied in place securely.

BONNET
Cut out fabric according to pattern piece. Neatly hem along the long front edge and two narrow sides that drop down from it, also hem along the bottom of section A.

Place the fabric wrong side down, with right sides facing.

42

Fold point A upwards and bring the side pieces up to meet either side of it. Pin or tack the joining seam and then sew in place. Turn right side out and add 10cm (4in) lengths of narrow satin ribbon to the front corners, so that the bonnet can be tied under the baby's chin.

LACE

Lace has been an important trimming and fashionable accessory since Renaissance times. It has been prized through the ages for its delicate, web-like appearance and worn by kings and queens including those on the throne today. The high, halo-like white collars worn by Queen Elizabeth I enhanced her image as the 'Virgin Queen'. The profusion of rich lace frills on the collars, knee-britches, handkerchiefs and cuffs worn by courtiers and kings in the reigns of Charles I and the French sovereign Louis XIV, highlighted their elitism, and wealth.

Traditionally lace was woven in silk or cotton, although threads of gold and silver have been used. In recent times man-made threads such as nylon have been introduced and where lace was once only made by hand on a lace-pillow using bobbins carved from wood, bone or ivory, machines have taken their place. Between the Renaissance and World War I, lace-making was an important industry, but with the advance of mechanization, lace has changed from being an indulgence of the wealthy to a high-street trimming.

There are many styles and types of lace, most named after the regions and countries where it is made. In England, Honiton and Nottingham lace are among the best known. Honiton lace is made in the area in and around the small south Devon market town of that name, where a handful of women still use the traditional skills.

LACE TAPE

Apart from tatting and bobbin lace, there is another type of lace made from special ribbon that can be gathered by pulling a thread sewn into the bottom edge of it.

Nottingham lace comes from a city in central England, where it is made in quantity, mostly by machine.

The lace-making regions of Chantilly in France and Flanders in Belgium are also renowned for their lace, as is the city of Limerick in Southern Ireland.

USING LACE TAPE

Draw a simple geometric or floral motif onto a piece of sturdy brown paper. This will act as a template. Using a fine lace ribbon or tape with the integral drawstring at the bottom of the ribbon, pin and tack in place over the template. Using the fine thread at the bottom of the ribbon, gather it neatly to fit round corners and arcs in your design. Sew the overlapping ribbon in place, so the motif is stable. Remove ribbon from the brown paper backing and transfer to where the decoration is to be attached. Sew in place.

QUILT-MAKING

QUILT-MAKING HAS NEARLY as many traditions and patterns as there are stitches in a quilt. There are examples of quilt-work, from cot-size to grand wedding quilts, dating back through centuries and from such diverse countries as the USA, France, Britain, India and Japan.

Currently popular and collectable are the quilts of the American Amish, a conservative religious sect which shuns adornment and does not use floral or patterned fabrics in sewing. Designs on Amish quilts are made up from the shapes of the fabric pieces and the order in which they are assembled. The quality of the handiwork is especially important, as the stitches stand out clearly on the plain fabric.

One of the oldest and most common quilting patterns is called A Trip around the World. The design is made by building up layers of identical squares, outwards from a central square. Other popular fabric shapes used to make designs are stripes, octagons and triangles. Leaves, petals, stars, hearts and human or animal figures can all be used to create picture quilts.

Domestic cottage quilts, called log-cabin work in the USA and Britain, were made for warmth and economy. Making them was a family affair, with husband, wife and children cutting and sewing the

QUILT ART

The amount of work that goes into designing, planning and sewing a quilt makes it a very special gift. The scraps of fabric used in the patterns may themselves carry fond memories.

shapes together. Traditionally, the pattern was built using strips around central squares of red fabric, which represented the hearth of the home.

Groups of neighbours, friends or relations would meet to make a quilt, using the scraps of fabric which were constantly being saved; great pride was taken in the quality of the work. These gatherings, called Quilting Bees, still take place in some small towns and villages, when commemorative or exhibition quilts are sewn.

Traditional wedding quilts are usually highly decorated, with patterns of the cornucopia horn of plenty, flowers, garlands, wreaths, doves and the tree of life. For the highly skilled needle-worker a pattern called the double wedding ring, made of intricate interlocking circles, is a test of patience and dexterity. Wedding quilts were often made from pieces of the bride's old dresses, so that the clothes she had worn through her childhood and adolescence became part of her wedding trousseau.

Although adult quilts were often stuffed with wool, those for children tended to be filled with cotton wadding, and in the Provençal region of France these small cotton quilts are called *boutis*. Popular motifs for nursery quilts are the alphabet, nursery rhyme pictures, sayings and mottoes.

Traditional shades of blue for a boy and pink for a girl combine to make a pretty pastel cot quilt. The use of both colours means that the cover can be used equally well for babies of either sex.

To make a plain quilt more special, details such as buttons, bows and ribbons can be added at the intersecting corners of each square quilt. A brightly coloured selection of buttons may also be sewn on to provide some visual entertainment for the baby.

SWEET DREAMS

A pillow with a traditional sampler-style alphabet decoration may be placed on a bed, cot or chair. The embroidery threads should be chosen to suit the decorative scheme of a room.

DESIGNING A QUILT PATTERN

Draw up a plan of your design on a sheet of graph paper and mark out the width and length of the quilt you wish to make, whether it is a small one for a baby's cot or a large one for a double bed.

It is traditional to create quilt patterns built around a regular block of patchwork squares, for example in groups of five, seven or nine. For a seven-patch block, the total number of squares making up the quilt would be 49.

Use each graph square to represent a square in the patchwork, and calculate the quilt measurements accordingly. Mark in, ideally with coloured crayons, where various colour changes and pattern variations will occur. This plan will provide you with a reference as you piece together your sewn squares. Quilts do not necessarily have to be made up from patchwork squares of different coloured fabrics. For the baby's quilt shown in the photograph, the same basic fabric is used for the whole of the quilt; pattern interest is created by varying the direction of the fabric stripes.

MAKING A PATCHWORK QUILT

There are many ways to make and sew a quilt; traditionalists maintain that hand-sewing is the proper way, but there are numerous short cuts, such as machine sewing, that can be used to save time.

MAKING UP SINGLE PATCHES OR SQUARES

Make a template or small paper pattern in the shape of a square and add a 6mm (¼in) seam allowance all the way around each individual square. Using the template, cut out accurate fabric squares and hem all the way around each shape. As a number of completed squares begin to accumulate, lay them out in sequence to form the desired pattern and carefully stitch the squares together to form a whole piece. It is advisable to press or iron each square as it is completed to ensure that you have a flat and even patch to work with.

BUILDING A PATTERN

A simple but classic pattern called the 'Chimney Sweep' can be created by following this plan:

Lay down one square to form a central point, then add another square to each of the four sides of the central square to form a cross shape. In between the arms of the cross, place four more squares, thus forming a larger square. In turn, more squares can be added row by row, to build up a full-sized quilt cover.

The completed quilt cover can be sewn onto a plain fabric backing, with an interlining of wadding placed between the two layers to give warmth and thickness to the quilt. The layers can be fixed using decorative techniques (see below).

MACHINE QUILTING USING SIMPLE SQUARES

The simplest method of making a quilt is to cut two pieces of fabric to the size of the desired finished quilt, plus seam allowances. Place one piece of fabric, right side down, on a flat surface and lay on top of it a layer of wadding or filling. On top of the wadding, place the other piece of fabric, right side up. Carefully align all three layers then pin and tack them together securely in closely spaced lines to form the verticals of the squares.

DESIGNING DETAILS

Quilt patterns can be created by carefully arranging the fabric squares according to where their printed motifs fall.

Fold the quilt in half lengthways to find the central line, then tack along it. Fold the two outer halves back into this centre line and again, where those lines form, tack along them so that the quilt is now divided into quarters. Repeat this procedure until you have achieved the number of lines that gives the quilt its required density. Turn the quilt widthways and repeat the same formula until you have completely sewn in all the squares. Following the tacked lines, machine stitch over them, making sure the stitches catch through all three layers of fabric.

FINISHING TOUCHES FOR QUILTS

If you make a patchwork quilt with an interlining and a fabric backing, a useful way of securing the three layers together is to add detailing at the corners of each patch shape or square.

TUFTING

When tufting it is best to use thick, sturdy cotton thread (crochet cotton is ideal). Using a double thickness, sew through from the front to the back of the quilt leaving a tail thread of about 3cm (1¼in) free on the top. Bring the needle back through to the top, and down again completing a whole stitch, then through to the back and up to the front again. Cut the thread, leaving a length that corresponds to the original tail thread. Tie the two ends together using a reef knot and neatly trim the ends to the same length.

BOWS AND APPLIQUÉ

As with tufting and buttons, daintily tied bows can be stitched to the corners of each patch or square (see detail of baby's quilt on page 46). Cut-out shapes and patterns can also be sewn onto the quilted background, for example a wreath or circlet of flowers, butterflies, simple heart shapes or plain strips of a contrasting material can all be overstitched onto a plain quilt.

ADDITIONAL ROWS OF STITCHING

Another way of creating an interesting border for a quilt is to add more rows of plain stitching. Two or three lines of closely sewn neat stitches will create a frame effect on the quilt and give it extra strength at the edges where the quilt is most handled and likely to become worn.

RAG DOLLS

A CHILD'S FAVOURITE DOLL OR teddy bear is very special and often becomes a memento that is kept throughout a lifetime. A number of famous bears belonging to presidents, prime ministers and royalty have crept out of the toy box and into the limelight in their owners' adult years.

Dolls have been around since at least the time of the Greeks and Romans. From the literature and art of the time it is known that both civilizations had jointed clay dolls; rag dolls date from Roman times. Girls in Greece were expected to sacrifice their dolls to Artemis, goddess of the Hunt, once they had been outgrown. Dolls of other cultures were crudely shaped from pieces of wood or corn stalks and representative of a god or spirit rather than used as a plaything, but in the eighteenth century glass-eyed dolls of heavy wood began to appear.

The advent of the wax doll brought a more attractive looking plaything to the nursery, but wax dolls tended to melt if they became warm, damaging easily with too much handling. The Victorian porcelain doll was slightly more robust and could be dressed in scaled-down contemporary clothes. The life-like doll gradually took shape, with its realistic painted face, real hair, eyelashes and rolling eyes that opened and closed as the head was rocked backwards and forwards.

RAG-DOLL TEA PARTY

These delightful rag dolls are equally charming as gifts for children or for adults and can be dressed accordingly.

RAG DOLLS

To make one doll:

MATERIALS

*One 30cm (12in) square of plain white
cotton for the body*

Kapok or similar soft fibre filling

*Embroidery threads for hair, face details
and shoes*

Fine muslin or gauze for underwear

Lengths of lace for trimming

Fabric for bonnet and dress

TO MAKE THE BODY

Trace out body shape onto plain white
cotton and cut out two body pieces. Place
right sides together and sew all the way
around, about 3mm (^{1}/$_8$in) in from the
edge, leaving a gap of about 6mm (^{1}/$_4$in)
under the arm. Turn right side out and
stuff with a soft fibre filling through the
gap. When the body is firmly filled, neatly
sew up the gap under the arm.

FACE DETAILS

With a soft pencil, lightly outline the position of the eyes, eyebrows, cheeks and
lips. Using a single strand of embroidery
silk, fill in the outlines with neat, tight
over-stitches. Add the hair by making
numerous tight French knots with thicker
lengths of embroidery silk or wool.

RAG DOLL CLOTHES

Trace and cut out pattern pieces (see page
122) in a fabric of your choice. Sew inside
out so that the seams are all on the reverse
side. Add trimmings of lace, bows and
buttons to suit the style of your doll.

PETTICOAT

MATERIALS

Cut 1 skirt

Cut 1 band top

Hem bottom of skirt and seam sides
together on the wrong side. Turn right
side out and sew a line of loose running
stitch along the top. Gather the top and fit
to the base of the band top, right sides facing. Sew in position so the seam is on the
wrong side. Turn right side out and fit on
doll then sew up back seam of top, add
ribbon shoulder straps and finish off with
bows or other decorations.

PANTALOONS

MATERIALS

Cut 4 leg shapes

Cut 1 waistband

*Cut 2 drawstring bands for pantaloon
legs*

Place together two leg shapes, wrong sides
facing and sew together the outside seams
(C) and (B) up to the gusset. Join the two
tube-like legs together by stitching round
the outside of the gusset. Turn right side
out. Place right side of the waistband
against right side of the top of the pantaloons. Fold the waistband over in half and
sew, leaving the ends open to receive the
drawstring. Repeat the waistband instruction for the drawstring casements on the
bottom of the legs (D). Thread fine elastic
or ribbon through the waist and leg casements on the doll and tie.

THE DRESS

MATERIALS

Cut 1 skirt

Cut 1 front bodice piece

Cut 2 back bodice pieces

Cut 1 front facing

Cut 2 back facings

Cut 2 sleeves

Cut 1 waistband

Hem the skirt, turn inside out and sew two
sides together. Hem base of sleeve and sew
a row of running stitches along the top;
gather to fit armhole. Turn wrong side out
and join the two sides together. Repeat for
other sleeve.

Stitch darts into place on front bodice,
keeping the tuck of material on the wrong
side. Place right sides together, sew the
front facing in place of the front bodice,
then turn back to the inside (wrong side)
of the garment, forming a neat edge along
the neckline. Repeat the same procedure
for the two sections of back bodice. With
right sides facing, place the back bodice
pieces in position on the front bodice. Sew
up the shoulder and side seams. Place the
lightly gathered sleeves in the armholes
and stitch in place.

With right sides facing, sew the waistband on to the gathered skirt so that the
seam is on the wrong side. Turn the completed bodice right side out and sew the
base of the bodice to the top of the waistband in the same manner as the skirt,
keeping the seam on the wrong side.

Slip the dress onto the doll and add a
button, catch or ribbon tie at the neck.

TRADITIONAL TOYS

IT IS KNOWN THAT CERTAIN toys were in existence in Ancient Greece and Rome, including hobby horses, hand carts and tops. Later, in the Middle Ages, childhood was not considered as a separate stage of life and children were expected to hunt and work alongside adults. Consequently the toys that were sold in fairs around the country differed little from those of hundreds of years before. There were still hobby horses, although they were more elaborately dressed, their bells and painted finery perhaps imitating the horses of jousting knights. Miniature farm animals were also popular, reflecting the mainly rural society, and tops and dolls were also commonly found.

In the eighteenth century a more liberal attitude towards childhood emerged. Initially, the new toys were mainly and obviously educational, such as jigsaws of complicated maps, but in Germany the toy industry was growing and, as the century progressed, elaborately painted wooden or metal animals, soldiers and miniature theatres began to appear across the world. Play for play's sake began to be recognized as important, having its own educational value.

It is from Germany that many of the more elaborate toys have originated, such as beautifully carved Noah's arks (which were only

NURSERY MAGIC

Traditional nursery toys have a timeless appeal, and remain popular. The sheep pull-toy (opposite) retains a period feel.

played with on sundays), and the more technical clockwork and mechanical figures. The famous German Steiff bear, with a hump between its shoulders, started the cult of the teddy bear, although the name teddy derives from that of the US president Theodore Roosevelt, who was famous for his bear hunting activities.

In the Victorian era, mechanical and balancing toys were popular, and puppets also became more widely available. Puppets from the

marionette to the glove puppet have a long tradition in many countries, whether as the form of entertainment seen in different countries' puppet theatres (such as the shadow theatres of India), or as individual toys. Jointed figures, such as monkeys and clowns, were worked by pulling strings, the basic models having single attachments to the legs and arms and the more elaborate figures having movement in most joints. Well-known European toy figures such as Harlequin and Punch and Judy owe much of their characters to the *Commedia dell'arte*, a sixteenth-century group of Italian actors who improvised plays from a stock cast of characters.

A puppet also appears inside the decorated case of the Jack-in-the-box and in the cone-on-stick, which conceals a figure that emerges from the centre of the cone when the stick is pushed upwards. It was from these early pop-up toys and string-pulled puppets that Automata figures, with moving parts, were developed. Automata were often used as childrens' saving boxes and, in 1873, the American Tammy Bank was patented. This portrayed the cast-iron figure of a man sitting in a chair. A coin placed in the man's hand caused his arm to counter-balance and tip up, dropping the coin into an opening (in some cases the figure's mouth), and hence into

SHEEP ON WHEELS PULL-TOY

MATERIALS FOR A SHEEP ON WHEELS

A display of materials for making the endearing sheep on wheels toy. From the nursery rhyme, Baa, Baa Black Sheep to its role in Christian imagery, the lamb is a popular symbol of innocence and childhood.

the body. The coin was stored there until the toy was turned upside down and the money was released through an opening in the base.

With the advent of the Industrial Revolution had come the mechanization of travel and the steam train. As a consequence, the toy train evolved. Initially the miniature versions were a crude imitation, but later they became more refined. The painted metal clockwork trains complete with tracks, signals, stations and passen-

LITTLE LAMB, WHO MADE THEE?

DOST THOU KNOW WHO MADE THEE?

GAVE THEE LIFE, AND BID THEE FEED,

BY THE STREAM AND O'ER THE MEAD;

GAVE THEE CLOTHING OF DELIGHT,

SOFTEST CLOTHING, WOOLLY, BRIGHT;

GAVE THEE SUCH A TENDER VOICE,

MAKING ALL THE VALES REJOICE?

William Blake

gers often became a hobby for adults as well as a plaything for children. Also copied from the real world were toy soldiers, with their forts and castles. Early lead soldiers are now collectors' items but their bright scarlet uniforms, black-painted bearskins or gold-crested hats and white trousers, once formed smart lines of mock-military defence and attack on the Victorian nursery floor.

Even in an age of computer games, traditional toys still have appeal.

MATERIALS

Length of cord 90cm (36in) long for pulling the toy

4 6cm (2¹/₂in) screws to attach sheep to base

12 4cm (1¹/₄in) screws to attach legs and neck to body

Wood adhesive

Stain or paint for legs and wheel base

Satin-finish varnish

BODY BASE

Cut a wooden figure-of-eight shape 31cm (12¹/₄in) long, 11cm (4¹/₄in) wide and 3.75cm (1¹/₂in) deep, (see pages 120 and 121 for template).

BODY AND HEAD STUFFING

Kapok or other similar soft-fibre filling

LEG SUPPORTS

4 pieces of dowel, each approximately 2.5cm (1in) in circumference, 17.5cm (7in) long, (including an allowance for recessing the legs into the base)

WHEEL BASE

Wood, 55cm (22in) long, 25cm (10in) wide and 2cm (³/₄in) deep

AXLE SUPPORTS

2 pieces of wood 25cm (10in) long, 3.75cm (1¹/₂in) deep

WHEELS

4, with a circumference of 10cm (4in)

SHEEP BODY FABRIC

1m (1yd) of 90cm (36in) wide bouclé fabric. For the face, use a 30cm (12in) square of woolly-type fabric.

TO MAKE SHEEP ON WHEELS

Use the pattern pieces on pages 120 and 121 to cut out wooden shapes for the base, legs, body base and wheels, and fabric shapes for the body, face and tail. The most suitable wood to use is softwood such as pine or deal. In addition to wood and fabric you will also need some embroidery thread to form the sheep's eyes (see photograph on page 53).

BODY BASE

Take the figure-of-eight piece of wood and form a table-like shape by screwing and gluing a piece of dowel in to each of the four corners as shown on the template. Countersink approximately 2.5cm (1in) of the dowel into the base and secure by screwing and gluing into the edge of the flat surface.

Sand the legs smooth to ensure that the 'table' shape stands evenly on all four legs. Paint or stain the legs and seal with a coat of satin varnish.

WHEEL BASE

Create a pointed end on the wood by cutting away the sides to form 14cm (5¹/₂in) shoulders on either side of a 7.5cm (3in) edge. Measure 2.5cm (1in) in from this narrow edge and drill a small hole, large enough to house a length of rope. Prepare the axles by screwing the wheels onto either end of the wooden struts. Screw on securely but allow the wheels to spin. Sand, stain and varnish all pieces.

SHEEP'S BODY

Pad above and below table-shape with foam and Kapok to form a sturdy but cuddly body. Place the two pieces of main body fabric right sides together. Sew along the top seam and half way down one side to the the tail position. Turn right sides out and lay on the body shape.

Attach the belly gusset between the legs at the tail point. Carefully stitching by hand, fit the sides of the gusset to the edges of the sheep's back. Add additional soft fibre filling or Kapok stuffing as you go, especially around the top of the leg joints. Finally, sew in the other end of the gusset to the bottom of the neck opening.

SHEEP'S HEAD

Sew on the eye details to the cut-out head shapes. Sew up face fabric, right sides together, leaving an opening for the neck. Turn right sides out and stuff firmly with Kapok or fibre filling. Place the head over the neck opening on the body, then sew on all the way around.

TO ATTACH SHEEP TO WHEEL BASE

Gently turn the sheep upside down. Rest the wheel base on top and mark the position of the legs. Drill out recesses in the base, about 2.5cm (1in) deep and line with wood adhesive; place legs in holes and allow to set. When adhesive is dry, secure fixture more firmly by screwing through from bottom of base and into legs.

TO ATTACH WHEELS

Turn the sheep, on its base, upside down and position the axle struts about 10cm (4in) in from the shoulder and bottom edges of the base. Attach with screws at regular intervals every 7.5cm (3in).

EARS AND TAIL

Sew the ears and tail pieces right sides together. Turn right side out and attach. Position ears evenly on either side of the head and gather as you sew to make them stand proud. Sew on tail and tie the towing cord to the base.

EASTER AND SPRINGTIME

EASTER'S ANCIENT AND PAGAN CUSTOMS were adapted and adopted by the Christian Church as a commemoration of the Resurrection. A movable feast, Easter Day is celebrated on the first Sunday after the full moon which occurs nearest to 21 March, the spring equinox.

Celebrations at this time of year also mark the changing of the season. The sounds of birdsong, the sight of bunches of flowers and the aroma of freshly baked spice- and fruit-filled biscuits and buns, make it a time that treats the senses.

LOVELIEST OF TREES, THE CHERRY NOW
IS HUNG WITH BLOOM ALONG THE BOUGH,
AND STANDS ABOUT THE WOODLAND RIDE
WEARING WHITE FOR EASTERTIDE.

A E Housman

EASTER TRADITIONS

ALTHOUGH EASTER AND springtime are traditionally times of joy and celebration, Good Friday, the day on which hot cross buns are customarily eaten, is intended to be a solemn occasion; a day of mourning for Christ's crucifixion. However, the spiced bread from which hot cross buns derive was once an important part of Anglo-Saxon pagan spring festivals and was eaten in hope of a good year to follow. The Ancient Greeks also ate similar buns, each adorned with a horned symbol as an offering to their goddess Eostre, while the Romans ate *Bonn* or *Bonus* for the festival of Diana. These incorporated an X inside a circle as a symbol of the sun and four seasons.

The cross on the buns has been adopted as a Christian symbol although, at one time, most buns carried this mark to help them rise during cooking. During the Reformation in England and the assertion of strong puritan values, Oliver Cromwell banned the baking of hot cross buns because of their pagan associations, but with the restoration of the monarchy the custom was revived.

Many lucky and curative properties have been attributed to hot cross buns. A few buns were set aside from a freshly baked batch and dried, until hard, in the oven, then strung up and stored in the

DELIVERING EASTER BUNS

A traditional Good Friday delivery of hot cross buns (above) and an array of edible Easter treats (opposite).

kitchen until needed. In this way the home would be protected and, if a member of the family was taken ill, the bun was crumbled into milk and used as a medicine.

In Sidmouth, a seaside town in Devon, England, hot cross buns are still given away free to local children on Good Friday. This ceremony began in 1898 when local bakers went on strike, and buns had to be rushed to the town from neighbouring villages, so that the good luck of the buns would still be passed amongst the townspeople.

Easter has long been a time for giving, as well as for ending feuds and old family differences. In the

English county of Hereford, three parishes conclude their Palm Sunday church service with the distribution of round pax or peace cakes, decorated with the motto *Peace and Good Neighbourhood* around a picture of the Lamb of God. The legacy is said to have been handed down from a Lady Jane Scudamore, who, in 1670, endowed money to provide cake and ale to promote peace and friendship.

Another springtime tradition is to bake and give a simnel cake for Mothering Sunday. The name of the cake is derived from the latin word *Simila*, and it is possible that similar cakes were baked in Roman times to celebrate the mother of the Gods.

In England, simnel cakes are supposed to be given on the fourth Sunday in Lent, although this is a period of fasting amongst strict observers. Today, the simnel cake is enjoyed over most of the Easter period.

Marzipan is the traditional covering for simnel cake, but many recipes include an integral layer of the sweet almond paste in the centre of the cake. On top of the cake, decoration is usually simple, just a number of rolled marzipan balls which can be egg-shaped. Some people choose to arrange 12 balls around the edge, signifying the 12 apostles, others leave the number at 11, omitting Judas, and a few opt for 13, to include Jesus.

EASTER CAKES

Simnel cake combines a delicious mixture of fruitcake and sweet almond paste. Traditionally eaten on Mother's Day, it is one of the few indulgences permitted during Lent time fasting.

SIMNEL CAKE

ALMOND PASTE
350g (12oz) ground almonds
350g (12oz) icing sugar
Yolks of 3 large eggs
2 teaspoons lemon juice
1 teaspoon pure almond essence
1 tablespoon brandy or sherry

CAKE MIXTURE
45g (1½oz) butter
20g (¾oz) white fat
65g (2¼oz) soft brown sugar
25g (1oz) ground almonds
3 large eggs
85g (3oz) plain white flour

A pinch of mixed spice
85g (3oz) currants
50g (2oz) sultanas
35g (1¼oz) raisins
15g (½oz) mixed peel
15g (½oz) glacé cherries (washed, dried and cut into quarters)

Preheat the oven to 180°C (35°F, gas mark 4). Grease and line a 15cm (6in) cake tin.

Beat together the butter, white fat, sugar and ground almonds in a bowl until light and fluffy. Beat the eggs and warm slightly in a pan over a low heat. Add the egg a little at a time to the cake mixture whilst beating constantly, until it is once again light and fluffy. Sieve the flour and spice into the mixture and fold in. Add the dried fruit and glacé cherries then stir until evenly distributed. Place half of the cake mixture in the prepared tin and set aside while you prepare the almond paste.

Make the almond paste by beating together the eggs, lemon juice, almond essence and alcohol. Place the almonds and icing sugar in a separate bowl and pour the liquid mixture over them. Mix and then knead together until a stiff but smooth paste is formed.

Roll out one third of the almond paste into a 15cm (6in) circle and place on top of the mixture in the tin. Top with the remaining cake mixture and flatten down with the back of a wet spoon. Bake in the centre of the oven for about an hour. Remember the centre of the cake is marzipan so the usual test for when the cake is ready (inserting a skewer into the cake) cannot be used. However, the cake is ready when it is springy to the touch and golden brown in colour.

When the cake has cooled, remove from the tin. Roll out two thirds of the remaining almond paste into a 15cm (6in) circle and place on top of the cake. Use all the remaining paste to make 12 evenly-sized balls and place around the edge of the cake. Toast the cake under a hot grill for a few minutes until the cake develops a slight golden tinge. Simnel cake makes a tasty and delightful gift for Easter or Mother's Day celebrations.

EASTER BISCUITS

Easter is a time for feasting after the long period of Lenten fasting. These biscuits are made from an old and enduring recipe that originates from Britain's West Country.

EASTER BISCUITS

Makes 24 biscuits

270g (9¹/₂oz) plain white flour
175g (6oz) butter
100g (4oz) caster sugar
50g (2oz) currants
1 egg
A pinch of ground nutmeg
A pinch of ground cinnamon
A pinch of mixed spice
Grated rind of 1 lemon
1 teaspoon lemon juice

Preheat the oven to 190°C (375°F, gas mark 5).

Place all the ingredients in a bowl and mix together until a smooth paste is formed. Roll out the paste on a lightly floured surface to a thickness of 6mm (¹/₄in) and cut out 5cm (2in) rounds. Arrange on a greased baking sheet and bake in the oven for 10 minutes. Sprinkle the biscuits with caster sugar while still hot and remove to a wire rack.

WRITTEN IN MARCH

LIKE AN ARMY DEFEATED
THE SNOW HAS RETREATED,
AND NOW DOTH FARE ILL
ON TOP OF THE BARE HILL;
THE PLOUGH BOY IS
WHOOPING-ANON-ANON:

THERE'S JOY IN THE MOUNTAINS;
THERE'S LIFE IN THE FOUNTAINS;
SMALL CLOUDS ARE SAILING,
BLUE SKY PREVAILING
THE RAIN IS OVER AND GONE!

William Wordsworth

HOT CROSS BUNS

Makes 30 buns

FRUIT MIXTURE
(Prepare a day in advance)
140ml (¹/₄pt) water
40g (1¹/₂oz) mixed peel
15g (¹/₂oz) cinnamon
15g (¹/₂oz) mixed spice
15g (¹/₂oz) ground ginger
50g (2oz) soft brown sugar
85g (3oz) currants
85g (3oz) sultanas

YEAST MIXTURE
450g (1lb) strong white flour
50g (2oz) caster sugar
50g (2oz) fresh yeast
500ml (1pt) warm milk
175ml (6fl oz) warm water

DOUGH
850g (1lb 14oz) strong white flour
175g (6oz) granulated sugar
175g (6oz) butter
2 eggs
A pinch of salt

CROSS DECORATION MIXTURE
175g (6oz) white flour
150ml (¹/₃pt) cold milk
40g (1¹/₂oz) vegetable oil
A pinch of baking powder

SUGAR GLAZE
4 tablespoons caster sugar
4 tablespoons hot water

EASTER FARE

*Hot cross buns are deemed to possess magical and medicinal
properties that bring good luck.*

To make the fruit mixture: bring the water to boiling point in a saucepan then add the sugar and spices. Bring back to the boil, remove from the heat and add all the dried fruit. Allow to cool, then place in an airtight container and leave overnight.

To make the yeast mixture: place all the ingredients together in a bowl and leave in a warm place to prove for 20 minutes.

Mix together all the dough ingredients then blend with the yeast mixture in a bowl, to form a smooth dough. Knead well on a floured surface. Cover the dough with a damp cloth and leave in a warm place for about an hour until it rises. Place the fruit mixture in a bowl and mix thoroughly by kneading the fruit into the dough. Once again, cover with a damp cloth and leave in a warm place to rise for about half an hour. Divide the dough into 30 evenly-sized pieces and mould into balls. Arrange them on greased baking sheets. Cover with a damp cloth and leave to rest in a warm place for 15 to 20 minutes until they have doubled in size.

Preheat the oven to 230°C (450°F, gas mark 8), then prepare the sugar glaze.

Make the cross decoration mixture by placing all the ingredients together in a bowl and stir until a smooth paste is formed. Use a piping bag to form a cross on each bun, then bake them in a hot oven for 10 minutes or until golden brown. Apply a thin layer of sugar glaze over them.

COATING FLOWERS

Coat freshly picked petals of primroses, violets, lilac, sweet peas or roses with a mixture of powdered gum arabic and scented rose water. Finished flowers will keep for several months.

PRIMROSE PETALS

Once crystallized, flowers can be used to decorate food – they are edible as long as the flowers you have chosen are safe to eat – and glued to ribbons for giftwrapping.

CRYSTALLIZED FLOWERS

Spring flowers are the first splash of colour to creep into frosty winter gardens. The most popular of these seasonal flowers are primroses and violets. The primrose grows wild in cool or mountain areas of the northern hemisphere, but can be cultivated in gardens. The name Primrose comes from the Latin – *Prima rosa* – meaning the first or earliest rose. The so called 'shy' violet, grows in small clumps and can be hard to find.

A way of capturing and preserving the beauty of these spring flowers is to crystallize the freshly picked blooms.

TO MAKE CRYSTALLIZED FLOWERS

50g (2oz) powdered gum arabic

4 teaspoons orange-flower water or rosewater

Fresh flowers: for spring, primroses and violets

For summer decoration try lilac, sweet peas, rose petals (ideal for wedding cakes) and for a blaze of colour, nasturtiums

Shake the powdered gum arabic into the scented water and leave overnight to dissolve thoroughly. Pick your fresh flowers just before you need them and make sure they are dry. With a small paint brush paint the gum solution evenly over the petals. Gently dip and sprinkle the flower with caster sugar, so that both the back and front have a light covering. Support the coated flower on a wire rack and leave to dry for at least 12 hours, until it is crisp to touch. Finished flowers can be stored for several months and are edible if your chosen flower is safe.

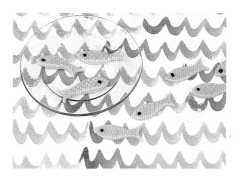

LOAVES AND FISHES

These marzipan fish can be toasted under a grill to give them a soft, golden-brown colouring.

MARZIPAN FISH

Fish have long been associated with the Christian festival of Easter. They crop up in many biblical stories and the symbol of the fish is a reminder of the miracle when Jesus preached the sermon on the mount and fed the five thousand from five loaves and two fishes.

Decorated fish-shaped biscuits and sweets are less common than the egg, but are nonetheless a traditional symbol for Easter-time celebrations.

Using your own home-made marzipan (see Simnel cake, page 60) or a good quality manufactured variety, roll out to approx 12mm ($^{1}/_{2}$ in) thickness on a board or table-top which has been lightly sprinkled with icing sugar. With an appropriately shaped biscuit cutter or sharp knife, cut out fish shapes and lightly criss-cross the top with a blade to create a scale-like effect. Add a currant for the eye. Brush sparingly with a fine layer of clear melted jam (apricot is ideal) and toast under the grill until slightly brown. Leave to cool on a wire rack.

EASTER EGGS

EGGS HAVE BEEN A SYMBOL of the spring calendar since pagan times. Long before the egg became a sign of the Resurrection, it was the fertility token of birth and growth. Chocolate, now a popular ingredient for the making of Easter eggs, was also associated with fertility and held to be of great value for its curative powers, by the Aztecs of South America. It was the Aztecs who gave the sweet brown substance its name from their word *xococatl – xococ* meaning bitter and *atl* meaning water.

The original Easter eggs that were given as gifts were ordinary birds' eggs, sometimes boiled in hot water to make them more robust, or blown, to empty out their contents. Modern designs are now applied with felt markers, ink or paint but in the past, natural dyes made from plants and insects – such as gorse flowers for yellow and crushed beetle shells for cochineal red.

Painted eggs are still exchanged between friends and families around the world. In Poland, eggs are painted red, blue and green in accordance with a legend that Mary did so to amuse the baby Jesus. The customary colour for dyed eggs is red. In Romania this is said to represent the blood of Christ; however in China, the colour red, like the egg, is used as a symbol of life.

In eastern Europe, egg decoration

EXCEPTIONAL EGGS

Easter eggs were traditionally carved from wood (above) or gathered from domestic fowl and decorated (right). Chocolate eggs became popular in the Victorian era.

is in fact a traditional peasant art. It reached its most refined form with the beautiful and expensive eggs designed by the Russian goldsmith and jeweller, Carl Fabergé, in the late nineteenth century. The most famous of these are probably the celebrated imperial Easter eggs, first commissioned way back in 1884 by Alexander III, for his Tsarina.

In Britain in the Middle Ages,

ordinary eggs were collected by the parish priest as his Easter tithe: some of these would then be blessed, and given as holy gifts. One of the earliest records of gifts of painted eggs in England dates back to 1290 when King Edward I distributed them to his household. The egg was probably then referred to as a paschal, using the ancient word *Pash* or *Paschal*, for Easter. In time, paschal evolved to the word pace, and in parts of the country, pace eggs are given at Easter.

Pace Egging, or knocking on neighbours' doors and chanting, was a traditional way for children to collect their eggs. Those they received were then either eaten or used in games. One ancient game still carried on today is egg rolling: eggs are tumbled, in a race, down a grassy bank; those that survive the ordeal are said to be blessed with luck. Egg rolling also takes place on the lawns of the White House in Washington DC; a tradition started by the wife of President Madison over one hundred years ago. The Christian custom of egg rolling is said to be symbolic of the moving of the boulder from the mouth of Christ's tomb on Ascension Day. Another game that has survived to the present day, is the Easter Egg Hunt, where eggs are hidden around the house or garden to be found by children.

DECORATIVE TECHNIQUES

The decoration of Easter eggs has evolved over the years to a point now when very few are done by hand. Most eggs are bought ready-formed and filled with commercially produced sweets. Originally Easter eggs were symbolic and decorative rather than edible, and were made of polished marble, wood or real birds' eggs.

Goose, duck and hen eggs can be hard-boiled in water for a semi-permanent decorative base or 'blown' clean of their contents for a longer lasting ornament. Blowing an egg is a task that demands great care and patience. The egg should be at room temperature, not taken from the fridge, and a small hole should be pierced with a darning needle at diametrically opposite ends of the egg. Carefully, over a bowl or basin, blow gently into the hole at one end of the egg and the contents should dribble out through the other end. When the egg is clear, gently rinse in warm water and allow to dry before starting to paint onto it.

It is best to paint straight onto an egg rather than draw a design on to it with a pencil, since the pencil lead tends to smudge on the eggshell and any unnecessary pressure may cause the egg to break.

A simple painted design can be made more exciting by gluing on sequins, beads, pearls and strips of ribbon or fabric. Other effects, such as batik-style wax-resist designs can be created by using melted candle wax or crayons to block out areas on the shell that should remain plain. The egg can then be completely covered in dye or paint and when dry, the wax removed to reveal the plain shell. If you wish to use several colours, keep patterns in one shade under wax while you dye other parts in different colours.

Paint effects also work well on a miniature scale; marbling, rag rolling, stencilling and sponging for example can all be used on eggs.

TO MAKE A CHOCOLATE EGG

Buy a plastic egg mould from a good kitchen shop and wash it well before use. Polish dry and make sure that it is completely free of dust or grease.

Melt some good quality chocolate (a good quality brand is less likely to crack when moulded) in a *bain-marie* or a heat-proof bowl resting in a pan of hot water. It is important that the water be neither too hot nor too cold as the chocolate could then form an ugly 'bloom' or opaque film on the surface.

When the chocolate has melted, pour on or paint on a thin layer of chocolate in the shells. Leave to cool and repeat the process several times until the shell is approx 6mm (¹/₄ in) thick. Leave in a cool place overnight, then carefully peel off the shell case and put the two halves together. Fillings such as home-made fondant creams, solid chocolate mini-eggs or candied peel may be used to fill the inside of the shell, and the sides can be joined together more securely by painting along the egg rims with a fine coating of warm melted chocolate, which will cool and firm like an adhesive. Decorate the outside of the egg with crystallized flowers (see page 63) and a wide satin bow or place it in a decorative box.

EASTER BUNNIES

The sweet, chocolate bunny found in shops at Easter has origins that date back to the pagan worship of a fertility goddess called Eostre, whose symbol was the hare or rabbit.

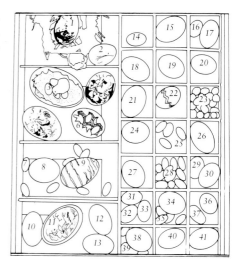

DECORATED EGGS PAGE 65

1 Antique guillemot egg in nest 2 Alabaster egg 3 Foil-wrapped chocolate eggs in card egg 4 Card egg 5 Card egg 6 Foil-wrapped chocolate eggs in card egg 7 Foil-wrapped chocolate eggs 8 Natural duck egg 9 Goose egg painted in watercolour stripes 10 Wooden egg 11 Old card egg 12 Wooden egg 13 Wooden egg 14 Painted wooden egg 15 Duck egg painted pink on blue 16 Painted wooden egg 17 Foil-wrapped chocolate egg 18 Wooden egg 19 Foil-wrapped chocolate egg 20 Hen egg painted red on blue 21 Duck egg painted with stripes 22 Hen egg painted yellow and green 23 Sugar-coated chocolate eggs 24 Natural hen egg 25 Foil-wrapped chocolate eggs 26 Decorated papier mâché egg 27 Hen egg painted blue on cerise 28 Foil-wrapped chocolate eggs 29 Painted wooden egg 30 Natural brown hen egg 31 Painted wooden eggs 32 Painted wooden eggs 33 Painted wooden eggs 34 Hen egg sprayed gold 35 Foil-wrapped chocolate eggs 36 Agate egg 37 Painted wooden egg 38 Hen egg painted, orange spots on red ground 39 Foil-wrapped eggs 40 Foil-wrapped chocolate egg 41 Painted hen egg.

SPRING TRADITIONS

AS A TIME OF BOTH REBIRTH AND renewal, Easter is connected with folklore related to planting. In Northern Ireland, there is a belief that if you plant potatoes on Saint Patrick's Day (17 March), you will have the first crop by the time the Orangemen march to celebrate the Battle of the Boyne (12 July).

In the past, Easter was the only time during the year that household fires were allowed to burn out. The hearth symbolized the heart of the home, and if the fire went out it meant bad luck, possibly death. In large houses and stately homes, Easter signalled a time of frenzied activity, as all the fires and stoves were put out and the chimneys and fireplaces cleaned. Spring is also the traditional season for baptizing babies and this is likely to have contributed to the belief that it was lucky to wear at least one item of new clothing for the first time at Easter.

1 May, also known as May Day, once marked the start of the Celtic new year, and still heralds the end of spring. May Day was originally celebrated as part of the Roman festival of Flora, held for the goddess of flowers and fruit. Dancing around the May Pole derives from these ancient fertility-cult dances and the name of the month comes from Maia, goddess of fertility and growth. Flowers at this time of year are still used in the day's festivities, to make garlands and wreaths.

SPRINGTIME BLOSSOMS

From the darkness of a dark cellar or garden shed, the first bright green shoots of spring appear. Bowls of bulbs planted in the autumn and winter herald the new season.

PLANTING BULBS

SPRING (FIRST VERSE)

SPRING GOETH ALL IN WHITE,
CROWNED WITH MILK-WHITE MAY:
IN FLEECY FLOCKS OF LIGHT
O'ER HEAVEN THE WHITE CLOUDS
STRAY:
WHITE BUTTERFLIES IN THE AIR;
WHITE DAISIES PRANK THE GROUND:
THE CHERRY AND HOARY PEAR
SCATTER THEIR SNOW AROUND.

Aubrey De Vere

ESTABLISHING THE BLOOMS

To make bulbs sprout quickly, place them in a cool, dark room, away from frost or excessive heat. As the pale, yellowish shoots appear and become established, remove to a lighter and warmer location. Watering may be required more frequently at this stage of growth.

MINIATURE BULBS

Miniature varieties of bulbs produce delicate and effective displays when planted up in containers. Suitable dwarf types of bulbs to use for indoor colour include:

IRIS

Miniature iris (Iris reticulata) in both blue and yellow, grows to a height of about 15cm (6in).

TULIPS

Miniature tulips: Tulipa greiggi is a long-lasting richly coloured tulip: Tulipa kaufmanniana is also known as the water-lily tulip and has wide, star-shaped pale yellow flowers with splashes of red; Tulipa tarda is a small yellow and white flower with five star-like petals.

DAFFODIL

Miniature daffodil (Narcissus cyclamineus) is a bright yellow variety indigenous to Spain and Portugal; its petals fold back, away from the trumpet of the flower in a distinctive shape.

HOW TO PLANT BULBS

Bulbs should be planted in a quality potting compost in a container that has good drainage and adequate room for root growth. The neck or sprouting tip of the bulb should be kept above soil level. Although it is essential for the bulb to receive moisture, take care to avoid over-watering and do not allow water to enter into the neck of the bulb as this could cause the inside to rot. Before watering, test the dampness of the compost with your fingertip – if the soil is still moist, do not water, but wait instead until it feels dry to the touch.

CONTAINERS

Although bulbs can be planted directly into decorative china containers or traditional terracotta pots (as long as they provide adequate drainage), it is often most practical to grow them in plastic plant pots. These rather mundane containers can be easily disguised and covered in a variety of ways to make them more presentable. For example, home-made cache pots created from folded cardboard or nailed lengths of hardboard can be decorated with Victorian style collages of paper cut-outs, sheets of pretty hand-printed paper or embellished with marbled or stencilled designs.

Baskets made from raffia or the more rustic style of woven twigs can be filled with a number of pots containing bulbs of different types. This is one way of presenting a collection of different-coloured bulbs in one container; as each type blooms and fades, the pot can be removed and replaced with a fresh one, giving a continuous display. The tops of the various pots can be covered with a thin layer of damp moss to give a more uniform effect.

A SEA OF COLOUR

Bulbs of the same shade and variety planted in a single container provide a vibrant splash of colour in the spring. In any case it is not advisable to plant different varieties of bulbs such as tulips and daffodils together in one pot, because as one flower comes into full bloom the other may still be a tight green bud. Eventually the display will be a sad and motley collection of blooming and dying flowers. Different colours of the same variety of flower are best grown separately for the same reason.

Other bulbs that are popular for both colour and scent are:

HYACINTH

Hyacinth (Hyacinthus orientalis) *hybrids, can be grown successfully in glass vases of water, although only the very base of the bulb should rest in the water. The intertwining white roots of the bulb make an additional point of interest.*

LILY OF THE VALLEY

Lily of the Valley (Convallaria majalis) *is traditionally given as a May Day gift in France.*

CROCUS

Crocus hybrids when presented growing in a pot can be placed outdoors and give a colourful and long lasting show, which is in contrast to the short life they have if cut, brought indoors and placed in a vase.

GRAPE HYACINTH

Grape hyacinth (Muscari armeniacum) *produces tiny, delicate bell-like flowers.*

CYCLAMEN

Cyclamen grown from a corm give colourful and long-lasting displays. Pots of cyclamen are best kept on a tray of small pebbles so that the roots sit above any excess water.

WEDDINGS AND ROMANCE

LOVE TOKENS EXCHANGED DURING COURTSHIP are invariably personal and decorative rather than useful, such as a flower or a piece of jewellery. In Wales the traditional romantic symbol is the wooden lovespoon, intricately and delicately carved. At one time its acceptance would have indicated engagement, giving rise to the word 'spooning', meaning courtship. A more widespread custom, associated with Valentine's day, is the giving of red roses. This is believed to have been started by Louis XVI of France, who sent them to his queen, Marie Antoinette.

I DREW MY BRIDE, BENEATH THE MOON,
ACROSS MY THRESHOLD; HAPPY HOUR!
BUT, AH, THE WALK THAT AFTERNOON
WE SAW THE WATER-FLAGS IN FLOWER!

Coventry Patmore from The Spirit's Epochs

BRIDAL GIFTS AND CUSTOMS

THE CUSTOM OF A BRIDE wearing *'something old, something new, something borrowed, something blue and a sixpence in your shoe'* is a chance for friends and family to give the bride an appropriate gift.

The garter is another traditional item, worn by the bride on the day of the wedding. Another custom is for the newly wed bride, on leaving the reception, to throw her posy of flowers to her unmarried girlfriends and her garter to the bachelors, those who catch the flowers and garter are said to be the next couple to announce their marriage.

The exchange of gifts of clothing between a courting couple was once considered too intimate to be allowed, but a Scottish bride would give her groom a shirt on their wedding night, with his initials embroidered on the hem; this was called a 'Wedding Sark'. Another Scottish custom is wedding bathing, which takes place on the night before the event. The bride-to-be is treated to a pleasant bath of scented water, but the prospective groom is covered, by his friends, in grease, ashes and soot. A ritual bath is also part of traditional Jewish weddings. Known as *Mikvah* such baths also take place before other important events. They are holy occasions involving the recital of prayers and are intended to cleanse and purify.

ROMANCE IN THE AIR

The engagement ring (above) is an official sign of the intent to marry. Specially made gifts for the bride may be given to her by close friends.

Most Christian weddings these days take place on Saturday, purely for the sake of convenience. In the past, the day was more likely to be dictated by the differing fortunes predicted for various days of the week, summed up in the rhyme: *'Monday for wealth, Tuesday for health, Wednesday the best day of all, Thursday for crosses, Friday for losses and Saturday, no luck at all.'* The season was also taken into consideration. Lent was an unlucky time of year for marriage, while autumn was lucky except during harvest-time, when all hands were needed to bring in the crops, so there was no time for celebrations.

The wedding dress is also the subject of many customs. Traditionally white to symbolize innocence and purity, the dress should be made *for* the bride and she should have no part in the process. A hair from the head of each person working on it should be sewn into the hem for luck. The wedding dress should not be completely finished until the wedding day, so the final stitches are often added while the bride dresses on the day.

It is thought unlucky to receive wedding presents that are sharp or pointed, so if a set of kitchen knives or cutlery is received, the bride should present a penny to the person who has given them, as in this way she 'buys' the gift and cheats bad luck. In Greece, it is the custom not to give the bride and groom presents, but to pin gifts of money to their clothes, as they dance at their wedding reception.

Wedding anniversaries are a time when a couple give gifts to one another in recognition of the years they have spent together. As the number of years increase, family and friends may be included in the anniversary celebrations.

PADDED COATHANGER

MATERIALS
Wooden coathanger

Strips of thin foam sheeting

Narrow ribbon to cover the hook of the hanger

A length of satin or other luxury fabric for hanger covering, approximately 15cm (6in) wide and three times the length of the hanger

Trimmings of lace and satin bows

Wrap strips of foam around the hanger to a depth of approximately 5cm (2in) and secure it by tying cotton thread around the hanger. To cover the hook of the coathanger, neatly wrap narrow ribbon

BRIDAL GIFTS
Useful and long-lasting bridal gifts include a scented, padded clothes hanger for storing the wedding dress (above) and a delicately-embroidered scented cushion (right).

A BALLAD UPON A WEDDING

HER CHEEKS SO RARE A WHITE WAS ON

NO DAISY MAKES COMPARISON,

(WHO SEES THEM IS UNDONE);

FOR STREAKS OF RED WERE

MINGLED THERE,

SUCH AS ARE ON A KATHERINE PEAR

(THE SIDE THAT'S NEXT THE SUN).

Sir John Suckling

around it. Secure by stitching the bottom of the ribbon to the foam padding on the hanger, and occasionally by sewing on the hook itself. Fold the fabric covering in half lengthways and cut a small hole in the middle of the folded top edge. Place the fabric over the hanger and stitch along the open bottom edge so that it is neat and fits closely to the edge of the padding. From each end, gather the fabric into small pleats so that it is the same size as the hanger. Stabilize the material by occasionally sewing the pleats in place to the foam backing. Fold over the open ends of the material or sew together neatly. Add lace, bows and other trimmings.

TO MAKE HEART-SHAPED SCENTED SACHETS

Using fabric such as satin or cloth sacking, cut out two heart-shaped pieces for each sachet. Embroider one of the pieces of

fabric with the initials of the bride and
groom, then add any other design or motif
you think appropriate. Place fabric right
sides together and sew up, leaving a small
gap. Turn right sides out and fill with dried
rose petals, lavender or camomile flowers.
Sew on lengths of ribbon to the top of each
sachet and tie to the hook of the hanger.

INITIAL CUSHION

MATERIALS
Two pieces of luxury fabric such as satin,
approximately 15cm (10in) square
Optional calico backing, same size as the
pieces above (only necessary if the outer
fabric is fine)
Length of fabric for frill, approximately
10cm (4in) wide and 90cm (36in) long,
hemmed along one edge
Embroidery threads for initials and
motifs on cover

Embroider initials or flowers on right side
of fabric that will form the top cover. (See
page 125 for an alphabet sampler.)

Gather and tack the frill on to the right
side of the bottom cover. Tack the frill
fabric in place with the turned edge placed
against the cushion and the unfinished
edge on the outside, allowing the unsewn
side to overlap the edge of the cushion by
approximately 1.5cm (¹/₂in).

Place the two right sides of the cushion
together, with the frill sandwiched between them. Sew through the three layers,
leaving an opening of approximately
10cm (4in). Turn right sides out, fill with a
soft fibre filling and sew up the opening.

COSMETIC BASKET

MATERIALS

A small open-top wicker or raffia basket

A small pot of emulsion paint in the colour of your choice

Fabric to line inside of the basket

Fabric to create the upper covering (plus an equal amount of material for the lining – approximately one and three quarter times the circumference of the basket)

A double length of cord or ribbon to gather closed the basket top

A narrow strip of fabric, same length as top covering and wide enough to take double thickness of cord

Paint the outside of the basket in a colour of your choice and allow to dry.

BASE LINING

Cut a circle of the lining fabric to fit generously into the base of the basket, and a similar piece with which to line the sides. Sew the bottom of the side lining to the edge of the circular base and fit neatly inside the basket.

Sew the top edge of the lining fabric to the upper rim of the basket to keep it in place, and add a few stitches through the base to anchor it.

TO MAKE THE BASKET TOP

Take the narrow length of fabric that will cover the tying-cord and sew the two long sides together to form a tube.

Place together the right sides of the lining and decorative fabric for the upper covering, and sew all the way around, leaving a small opening. Turn the fabric inside out and sew up the opening. Add lace or other trimming to the top edge of the material.

Sew the narrow tube of fabric through which the tying cord will run, to the right side of the upper covering. Cut and oversew two openings through which the cord can be pulled.

Carefully tack the bottom edge of the upper covering in position on the upper rim of the basket, gathering and pleating as you go so that the fabric fits snugly to the basket. Sew in place and join the remaining open sides together.

Thread the cord through the tube opening twice and knot or sew the two ends together securely. Pull alternate loops through opposite holes so that the fabric gathers close. Pull opposite cords to open the basket.

Fill the basket with small gifts for the bride, such as a bottle of *eau de cologne* or lavender water, an embroidered pin cushion or a handkerchief and a sachet of bath herbs.

A BRIDE'S TROUSSEAU

A bride-to-be's wedding trousseau, known in France as a dot, normally consisted of clothes and linen to be taken to her new home. Gifts commonly associated with a trousseau may include elaborate coathangers or delicately embroidered cushions. (right) Here a plain basket has been transformed into a stylish dressing-table accessory for a bride. Filled with favourite soaps or bath oils, a bridal basket makes a special, personal gift.

SAMPLERS AND NEEDLEPOINT

SAMPLERS HAVE A LONG AND important history as chronicles of the social and domestic times in which they were made, and as records of family names and dates. They were so named because they were sewn by young girls who made up patterns from samples of different types of stitches they had learned. Popular sampler decorations included the maker's name, the date on which the sampler was completed, a religious or moral motto and a patterned border. Samplers were also sewn as gifts to commemorate a date or event such as a wedding or a birth, with the initials or names of the bride and groom, or parents and child, worked into the pattern – an ideal way of making a personal and special gift.

In Elizabethan times, needlework was more than a pastime, it was an important part of a girl's education. Needlework finely sewn in the sixteenth century by Mary Queen of Scots and Bess of Hardwick, can be seen to this day at Oxburgh Hall in Norfolk, England. Their work features heraldic animals, mottoes and titles in Latin.

Embroidery was not just worked on wall-hangings and cushions, it was also fashionable for giving richness and texture to court and formal clothing. Stomachers, the stiff triangular panels worn at the front of the dress-bodice, were a popular

A STITCH IN TIME

Needlework samplers make gifts that may be treasured for years to come. Dates, names or initials personalize a sampler and add historical interest.

area for the application of rich decoration, as were the cuffs of gloves, toes of shoes and the ankles of a gentleman's stockings. Boxes and trinket cases were also elaborately dressed up with fine needlework in gold and silver thread. The earliest dated example of an English sampler was worked by a young girl in 1598. In it are many threads of silver and gilt, as well as coloured silks.

Decorative needlework underwent a revival in Victorian times when it was used extensively about the home, on fire-screens, chairs and footstools, and on clothes, such

as slippers, bags and purses. Needlework during this period was much influenced by the Arts and Crafts movement and its chief protagonist William Morris, who revolutionized the art of house decoration and furnishing in England and elsewhere. Many of his designs had an early, medieval quality in their style and richness of colour, which adapted well to needlework.

Sampler motifs and designs tend to reflect the location of the maker. Colonial American samplers may incorporate a traditionally dressed couple with the man in breeches and tricorn hat, and the wife in a full length skirt and apron, surrounded by finely sewn borders of strawberries and native flowers.

However, a needlewoman in a religious community of American Shakers would use a motto as the centre piece to her sampler, such as: *Put your hands to work and your hearts to God.*

Samplers can be dated by their style of decoration. The Victorians favoured highly ornate designs with bows, clusters of fruit, berries and bunches of flowers, while earlier work from rural communities is naïve in style, with a simple and uncluttered appearance. Old samplers have now become valued and collectable items, with high prices being obtained at auctions.

TRADITIONAL SAMPLER

NEEDLEPOINT SAMPLER

Finished size of sampler design:
25 × 33cm (10 × 12½in)

MATERIALS

*Mono de luxe canvas 18 holes to the
inch, 35 × 42.5cm (14 × 17in)*

Size 22 needle

Masking tape to bind edges

Sharp scissors for cutting canvas

Embroidery scissors

Appletons crewel wool in skeins:

Colour number	Description	Skeins
714	Dark plum	1
712	Light plum	1
295	Dark green	2
292	Pale green	2
353	Grass green	2
903	Ochre	1
693	Gold	1
224	Dark rose	2
222	Pink	2
881	Background	13

THE CANVAS

The canvas does not have to be marked out; instead, just follow the colour chart opposite. Remember that each square represents one intersection of canvas thread and not the hole between the thread. Each square represents one tent stitch (see diagram below). Before beginning to stitch, it is advisable to mark the top of the canvas, so that if you turn the canvas while stitching you will know where the top is. Please note that the colours on the chart are stronger than the

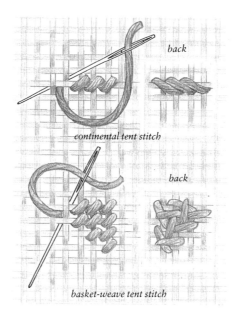

continental tent stitch

back

back

basket-weave tent stitch

NEEDLEPOINT STITCHES

*Details and instructions of stitches recommended
for use when sewing the needlepoint sampler.*

A LITTLE DAILY EMBROIDERY
HAD BEEN A CONSTANT
ELEMENT IN MRS TRANSOME'S
LIFE; THAT SOOTHING
OCCUPATION OF TAKING
STITCHES TO PRODUCE WHAT
NEITHER SHE NOR ANY ONE
ELSE WANTED, WAS THEN THE
RESOURCE OF MANY A WELL-
BORN AND UNHAPPY WOMAN.

George Eliot, Middlemarch

wools themselves, to make them easier to see. The corresponding wool colours are on the colour key.

HOW TO STITCH

Work the sampler in tent stitch (see below) using two strands of wool. Cut the canvas to size and bind the edges. Begin in any area you wish, although it may be easier to start at the top right-hand corner and work in blocks of colour. Leave the background to last.

TO PERSONALIZE

Before working the background, and using the colour photograph as a guide, personalize your design with your own initials and the year in which you made it, tracking them through onto your canvas with an HB pencil or permanent marker so that they are easily visible when stitching.

MAKING UP

Stretching: When you have finished your design, the needlepoint must be 'square' before framing. If out-of-square, the tapestry should be lightly dampened or sprayed and left for a few minutes so that the canvas softens. Gently pull square and then pin out, right side down, into blotting paper on a flat, clean board. Use tacks, staples or drawing pins and pin outside the sewn surface. Do not strain too tightly or the tapestry will dry with a scalloped edge. When thoroughly dry, remove from the board. The drying process may take 2–3 days and sometimes it is necessary to repeat the process.

Framing: You may prefer to take your tapestry to a professional framer who will be able to stretch the canvas for you as well as frame the finished tapestry.

FLOWERS

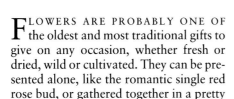

FLOWERS ARE PROBABLY ONE OF the oldest and most traditional gifts to give on any occasion, whether fresh or dried, wild or cultivated. They can be presented alone, like the romantic single red rose bud, or gathered together in a pretty bouquet or posy.

Queen Victoria's own wedding bouquet contained sprigs of myrtle, the flower of love, which subsequently became a very popular addition to other types of posies. A tussie mussie in Tudor times might have contained marigolds, green broom and rosemary, gilded with gold leaf and dipped in scented rose water, for extra potency. Since Roman times, nuts have been a symbol of fertility, and a bride in Devon, England, might still find twigs of hazelnuts in her bouquet. The continental custom of giving little parcels of sugared almonds to wedding guests, springs from the same belief.

The Greeks held japonica as a promoter of love, and in Germany, lime flowers were kept out of the homes of young women because their heady scent was thought to promote erotic dreams. Honeysuckle and the equally heavily scented lily of the valley are also regarded as love charms. French brides often include mignonette, also known as 'my little darling' in their posies as a charm to hold their husband's affections.

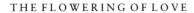

THE FLOWERING OF LOVE

Superstitious people believe that snowdrops should not be brought indoors, but they make a delightful springtime posy.

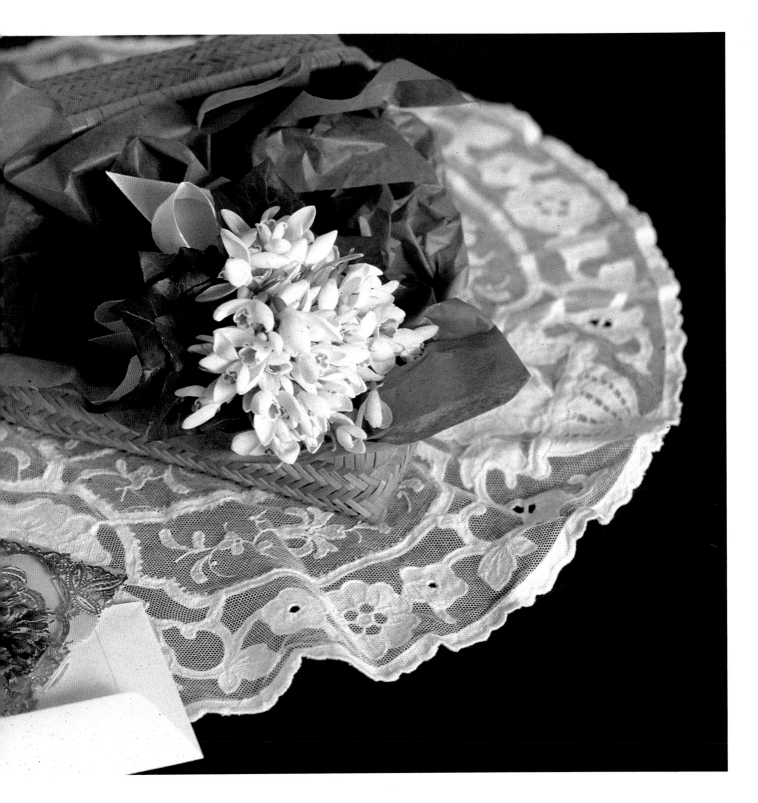

THE LANGUAGE OF FLOWERS

ROSES

Roses are usually accepted as being the universal symbol of love, but there are a multitude of varieties of the flower, and many of them have other meanings. The red rose, for example, has been attributed with a number of symbolic meanings. As a bud, it is straightforwardly a sign of purity and love. The deep red flower, however, alludes to bashfulness and shame but is also, as a result of its use as the emblem for the House of Lancaster during the English 'War of the Roses', a symbol of war. This, of course, is equally true of the House of York's white rose, although the bud again has a different meaning of youth and innocence.

MARIGOLDS

Marigolds, despite their cheerful appearance, have mainly unhappy associations, with the French variety indicating jealousy and the African, vulgarity. In general, the marigold serves as an omen, predicting the need to watch out for future events.

TULIPS

Tulips, like other flowers, mean different things according to their colour – the beautiful bright red form of the flower declares love, and the yellow colour once more has a negative connotation; in this case, hopeless love. A tulip with variegated petals tells the recipient that they have beautiful eyes.

CARNATIONS

Carnations are scented and colourful flowers which have a range of meanings and implications. Red carnations tell the woeful tale 'Alas for my poor heart'. The same flowers in shades of yellow, denote disdain, while the striped variety signifies a refusal. The smaller carnations or pinks carry messages of love and aspiration.

CHRYSANTHEMUMS

Chrysanthemums, from the daisy to the Pom Pom, are popular autumnal flowers and the white flower, a symbol of truth, is frequently used in ceremonial and formal arrangements. As with all flowers, the meaning depends upon colour and variety. The Chinese chrysanthemum is a recognition of cheerfulness under adversity, but the red flowers, like the red rose-buds, are a declaration of love. However, yellow once again has a negative overtone of slighted love.

DAISIES

Daisies come in many varieties, both wild and cultivated; each has its own connotations. The garden daisy carries the message 'I share your sentiments', and similarly the double daisy can be taken as a sign of participation or involvement. The gift of red daisies, unusually, asks a question – is the recipient aware of the giver's emotions? A return gift of a wild daisy shows that the question is being considered.

GERANIUMS

Geraniums, except for the darkest red bloom which signifies melancholy, are well-meaning, with a generally positive message. As a bridal favour, the ivy geranium is popular in wedding bouquets. However, other varieties would be equally appropriate: the oak-leaved geranium as a sign of true friendship, or even the pink-coloured flowers, implying preference. Both scarlet and silver-leaved geraniums would have a different purpose; the former as an assurance of comfort, the latter as a memory recalled.

JASMINE

Jasmine is usually valued for its scent, but again it is the colour and variety of the jasmine flower which determines its message. If white, it is a sign of amiability; if yellow, grace and elegance. Each variety carries very different implications; the Carolina warns of separation, whereas the Indian reveals attachment – two contradictory meanings.

LILIES

Lilies are flowers that drift in and out of favour with changing fashions. The white trumpet lily, once popular as a wedding flower in the 1920s, has since become a symbol of death and is now used more often at funerals. Although lilies are in general a symbol of purity, the Day lily is, by contrast, a sign of coquetry.

FLORAL ARRANGEMENT

The tussie mussie is an attractive way of creating a hand-held posy. Concentric circles of colourful and scented flowers form a dainty display.

LOVE IS IN THE AIR

Flowers have long been associated with romance and betrothal and many flowers have special significance for lovers.

LOVE LETTERS

Lovers' notes say much with words, but when accompanied by a thoughtfully selected array of flowers, the message carries extra meaning.

TUSSIE MUSSIES

FOR A DRAMATIC DECORATIVE effect, these hand-held Victorian-style posies should be assembled in several concentric circles of colour. Start with a small bunch of one type of flower in the centre and build outwards with other flowers of contrasting or complementary shades. The final, outer layer should be made up from foliage to form a delicate, and effective frame.

Secure the tussie mussie by tying the flower stems together using twine that has been covered with decorative ribbon, then finish off the posy with a generous bow. The ends of the flower stems should be cut neatly to the same length, and if the posy is

THE FLOWERS

BUY MY ENGLISH POSIES!
KENT AND SURREY MAY –
VIOLETS OF THE UNDERCLIFF
WET WITH CHANNEL SPRAY;
COWSLIPS FROM A DEVON COMBE –
MIDLAND FURZE AFIRE –
BUY MY ENGLISH POSIES,
AND I'LL SELL YOUR HEART'S DESIRE

Rudyard Kipling

to be presented some time after it is made, wrap the stems in some damp newspaper to keep the flowers fresh.

FLOWER COMBINATIONS FOR A SPRINGTIME TUSSIE MUSSIE

Neatly bunch together in your hand eight or nine double narcissi to form the centre of the posy. One by one, and turning the posy as you go, add pink- and bluebells until a complete circle has been achieved. In a similar way, add a selection of pale pastel bud tulips to create a third ring, and finally add a partially overlapping band of large green leaves. Tie neatly with cord, trim stems to an even length and cover the cord with a wide length of wire or pastel satin ribbon to neaten.

CUSHIONS

CUSHIONS MAKE BOTH DECORA-tive and practical gifts. Indeed, in some cultures such as that of the nomadic Bedouin Arabs, cushions are an important piece of furniture. The word cushion comes from the middle English word *cuisshen*, which in turn owes its origin to the Old French *coissin*, meaning a hip rest.

In the past ornamental cushions were a symbol of wealth and status, as only people who had the time and money to lounge around had need of them. Kings and emperors were frequently surrounded by piles of brilliantly coloured and intricately stitched examples. In Asia, especially China with its important silk industry, fine and exotic embroidery was used to decorate cushions; magnificent examples were worked with gold- and jewel-coloured threads into fanciful shapes of fire-spitting dragons and mythical figures.

The type of decoration that can be applied to a cushion is almost without limit – patchwork, embroidery and tapestry are all favoured mediums. The currently popular Borgello Florentine type of needlework, using dense stitching in shaded colours of wool, is said to have been brought to Italy during Renaissance times by the Hungarian bride of one of the Medicis, and makes a sturdy and attractive cushion cover.

The stuffings and fillings of cushions were also regarded as important and in medieval times, mattresses were stuffed with straw and handfuls of herbs, some appropriately named, such as Lady's bed-straw. For people who had trouble sleeping or suffered from asthma, cushions filled with hops were advised. As a relief for headaches, dried lavender flowers, lemon balm, lemon thyme and peppermint leaves were prescribed.

ALPHABET CUSHION

A sampler-style cushion cover using letters, initials and insignia to form a pattern. This style of decoration will look best if worked in a single colour.

HOW TO MAKE A HERB PILLOW

Herb cushions and pillows can be made to fulfil a variety of purposes. A filling of dried hops with a little lavender makes a comforting and sleep-inducing headrest and handfuls of dried golden feverfew mixed with bergamot will create a cushion that helps to relieve headaches. Cushions can also be tailored to suit the needs of a family pet. A mat for a kennel or cat's basket, stitched with a filling of lemon verbena, will help to reduce 'doggy smells'.

Mint helps to keep flies away and southernwood, traditionally used as a worm remedy, will help to keep the family hound sweet. For feline pets, there is nothing quite like a cushion filled with catnip, a herb which most cats find totally irresistible.

Basic rules for making herb cushions and pillows are that the herbs you choose should be well dried and crumbled (but not so small that they turn powdery), then securely sewn into a lining of muslin or fine gauzy cotton. To prevent the dried contents from being too crackly, add a

88

HERBAL CUSHIONS

Herb and spice cushions can be filled with your own combination of petals and leaves to give a unique scent.

HERB MIXTURES

CUSHION LINING

A fine cotton lining bag allows scent to pass through.

HEADACHE CUSHION

For a headache cushion, mix together equal quantities of bergamot, lemon verbena and mint. For the mint, use a selection of varieties such as lemon mint, spearmint and peppermint. Add one tablespoon of crushed orris root as a fixative, to prevent both decay and the fading of the scent. Put the mixed herbs into a partially-sewn cotton lining case and complete the last seam, then place inside a decorative outer cover.

SPICE CUSHION

For a spice cushion, combine equal amounts of rose petals and lavender with a few crushed cloves, slivers of nutmeg and a pounded cinnamon stick for an aromatic treat.

SCENTED BAGS

Scented sachets for clothes drawers and coathangers can be filled with herbs that combine scent with useful properties.

few drops of floral oil for example. In a sleep-cushion, drops of lavender or rose oil will help. The outer covering of the cushion can be as plain or as fancy as you like, but it is best to avoid heavy and densely woven fabrics which might hinder the scent from permeating through.

HERBAL CUSHION DECORATIONS

Herbal cushion covers may be decorated in a variety of ways, including embroidery, appliqué or painting. In keeping with traditional ideas, it may be appropriate to apply a botanical illustration of the cushion's contents using one of the methods mentioned below.

Botanical drawings include not only a flower and its leaves, but also details of its root structure and the appropriate fruit and buds, together with its Latin name.

To transfer a herb illustration on to a cushion, trace and simplify, if necessary, the desired herb from a reference book then transfer it on to a plain calico cotton cover. Fill in the outlines with fine overstitching using rich silk embroidery threads or painted on the outlines.

CHRISTMAS AND THANKSGIVING

THE FINAL MONTHS OF THE YEAR ARE full of celebrations. Christmas is a widely observed festival, involving not just religious celebration but the exchange of presents and feasting on seasonal foods. It is a time surrounded by many tales and traditions.

Thanksgiving is a time for celebrating the first successful harvest brought in by English and Dutch settlers, after their arrival in the New World. The food eaten at this festival represents the produce which was originally grown successfully by the first settlers, including pumpkins and cranberries.

'WE'LL TO THE WOODS NO MORE,
THE LAURELS ARE ALL CUT.'

A E Housman

PLUM PUDDING, MINCE PIES AND SAUCES

PREPARATIONS FOR CHRISTMAS feasting traditionally start on Stir-up Sunday, the Sunday before the beginning of Advent in early November. This is the time when cakes and puddings are prepared, and every member of the household stirs the bowl of ingredients and makes a wish. Silver sixpences or tokens such as a thimble (for an old maid) and a wishbone (for luck) are added, to be found later when the cooked pudding is eaten. These tokens may have evolved from the pea or bean hidden in Twelfth Night cakes, which are still served in France today.

Christmas cake was originally known as Plumb cake, it was made with butter raisins known as plumbs, and decorated with sweet paste called *marchpane*, the forerunner to marzipan. It is thought very unlucky to bring a cake or pudding to the table 'undressed', so marzipan, or at least a sprig of holly, should be placed on top. Not all nationalities favour heavy fruit cakes. In Italy, and particularly in Milan, a lighter raised yeast and fruit cake called Pannetone is eaten.

From Yorkshire in the north of England comes a spicy fruit bread called the Ripon Yule log. Customarily eaten with a slice of cheese, fruit cakes have always been very popular in Yorkshire. They were an ideal way for traditionally thrifty

FESTIVE FOOD

Stir-up Sunday (above) begins the seasonal food preparations. Plum pudding (right) is enlivened with frosted cranberries.

Yorkshire housewives to make the most of the heat in the oven after cooking a meal; the oven temperature was turned down, and as it cooled, the cake or loaf was put in to bake slowly.

French families favour a chocolate or chestnut yule log cake, covered with chocolate icing and sculpted to look like the bark of a tree. The yule log cake is based on a pagan custom which survived until recently in Scotland. The yule log called the *Caileeach Nollaich* (old

woman) was a large piece of oak or ash, or a fruit tree, decorated, and sometimes with the face of an old woman carved to represent the past year. The log was dragged home and put on the hearth-fire where, according to folklore, it had to be totally consumed by fire, otherwise bad luck would follow in the new year. The Scots, however, do not eat sweet yule log cake, instead they eat slices of Black Bun, a rich treacle, fruit, spice and nut cake baked like a pie with pastry crusts and accompanied by a dram of whisky.

In medieval times, plum porridge or pottage was made from leftovers of meat, currants, raisins, prunes, spices and claret. This meaty mixture was the forerunner to our mincemeat, although the only remnant of the meat in modern recipes is suet. Originally, mince pies were made in an oval shape, known as a coffin, to symbolize Christ's crib. It was supposed to be lucky to eat a pie a day, each made by a different person, for the twelve days immediately preceding Christmas.

The traditional accompaniment to Christmas pudding is brandy butter, sometimes called King George's sauce. Similar to brandy butter are guard sauce (the basic mixture has ground almonds added and is whipped to a cream-like consistency), and Cumberland butter, where rum is used to add flavour.

CHRISTMAS PUDDING

225g (8oz) raisins
70g (2¹/₂oz) currants
45g (1¹/₂oz) mixed peel
35g (1¹/₄oz) glacé cherries
35g (1¹/₄oz) sultanas
15g (¹/₂oz) flaked almonds
50g (2oz) suet
45g (1¹/₂oz) white breadcrumbs
45g (1¹/₂oz) plain flour
70g (2¹/₂oz) dark brown sugar
A pinch of mixed spice
A pinch of nutmeg
2 eggs
3 tablespoons ale or beer
3 tablespoons brandy
4 teaspoons fresh lemon juice
4 teaspoons fresh unsweetened orange juice
40g (1¹/₂oz) baking apple
30g (1oz) carrot

This recipe will make one 900g (2lb), two 450g (1lb) or four 225g (8oz) puddings
  Peel, core and finely grate the apples and grate the carrots. Place the dried fruit, almonds, suet, breadcrumbs, flour, sugar and spices into a mixing bowl then add the apple and carrot. Mix together until well distributed. Add the egg, fruit juices and alcohol and stir with a wooden spoon until the mixture binds together.
Place the mixture in a pudding basin, and flatten down evenly. Place a circle of greaseproof paper over the top of the mix-ture and then cover the basin with a piece of cloth, tying a piece of string around the rim to secure it. To help you lift the basin easily, make a handle by bringing the loose ends of the cloth over the top of the basin and tying them together. Put a trivet in the bottom of a large pan and lower the pudding basin on to it. Pour boiling water into the pan until the pudding basin is two thirds immersed. Cover the pan and sim-mer the pudding for about 9–10 hours, adding more boiling water as necessary.
  Remove the pudding from the pan,

PLUM PUDDINGS

Bowls filled with rich Christmas pudding wait to be boiled, which can take the best part of a day. Cooked pudding can be served with rum butter and frosted cranberries.

using the tied ends of the cloth as a handle. Uncover the pudding and unmould it from the basin. Just before serving, pour a small glass of warmed brandy over the top and hold a lighted match near the pudding to ignite the brandy.

SWEET MINCEMEAT

225g (8oz) cooking apples, peeled, cored
and chopped
100g (4oz) suet
100g (4oz) raisins
75g (3oz) sultanas
50g (2oz) orange peel
50g (2oz) lemon peel
1 teaspoon candied citrus peel
175g (6oz) currants
75g (3oz) soft brown sugar
A pinch of salt
A pinch of ground cloves
A pinch of ground nutmeg
A pinch of ground cinnamon
A pinch of ground mixed spice
25g (1oz) glacé cherries, chopped
15g (^{1}/$_2$oz) glacé ginger, chopped
30ml (1fl oz) rum
15ml (^{1}/$_2$fl oz) brandy
15ml (^{1}/$_2$fl oz) lemon juice

Prepare the apples, cherries and ginger, then add all the fruit to the suet, spices and sugar. Mix together all the ingredients with lemon juice. Place in a container then pour over the rum and brandy, cover and leave to allow the alcohol to soak into the fruit. Marinate for two weeks before use.

CHRISTMAS MINCE PIES

Mince pies can be made with short-crust or flaky pastry. Short-crust pastry can be enhanced by adding ground almonds and reducing flour.

RUM SAUCE

100g (4oz) butter
100g (4oz) plain white flour
1.1l (2pts) milk
150ml (5fl oz) rum
100g (4oz) soft brown sugar

Melt the butter in a saucepan, add the flour and stir over a low heat with a balloon whisk to make a pale roux. Very slowly add the milk, a little at a time, stirring continually and cooking after each addition. Stir in the sugar and continue to cook over a very low heat for ten minutes, stirring constantly. Add the rum and taste to check sugar and alcohol levels then keep warm until served.

RIPON YULE LOAF

Makes two loaves

200g (7oz) strong plain flour
A pinch of salt
A pinch of cinnamon
1 teaspoon mixed spice
40g (1^1/$_2$oz) caster sugar
60g (2oz) white shortening
160g (5^1/$_2$oz) currants
130g (4^1/$_2$oz) sultanas
40g (1^1/$_2$oz) raisins
20g (^{3}/$_4$oz) mixed peel
1 egg yolk

YEAST MIXTURE

15g (^{1}/$_2$oz) caster sugar
30g (1oz) fresh yeast
50g (1oz) strong plain flour
200ml (7fl oz) milk (tepid)

Preheat oven to 200°C (400°F, gas mark 6). For the yeast mixture: dissolve the yeast in the milk and put in a bowl with the sugar and flour. Mix together, cover and leave to stand in a warm place until frothy.

Place all the other ingredients in a separate bowl and add the fermented yeast mixture. Mix together until a smooth, manageable dough is formed, adding extra flour if necessary. Knead the dough on a floured surface until smooth and silky in texture. Divide into two equal pieces and mould each into a loaf shape. Place in greased 450g (1lb) loaf tins. Cover tins and leave to prove, then bake in an oven for 25–30 minutes.

NEEDLEPOINT STOCKINGS

STOCKING FILLERS

*A stocking filled with gifts brings excitement to all children on
Christmas mornings.*

THE CUSTOM OF 'HANGING up a baby's stocking' is thought to have originated from the story of Bishop Nicholas on whom the Father Christmas legend is based. The story tells how a local nobleman had lost his fortune and was sadly unable to provide dowries for his three unmarried daughters. So one night Bishop (and later Saint) Nicholas threw three purses of gold through the front door of their home and they landed in stockings that were drying in front of the fire. Saint Nicholas, because of this story, is also the patron saint of pawnbrokers, hence the three gold balls of their sign, representing the three bags of gold.

Children, of course, do not now necessarily hang their stocking over the fireplace but put it out ready for Father Christmas's arrival, traditionally down the chimney. They also leave out mince pies and sherry for him to eat. In Britain and North America, this procedure has long been part of every excited child's ritual in anticipation of Christmas Day morning.

In the nineteenth century, mothers elaborated on their children's mundane cotton or woollen everyday stockings by embroidering them, with intricate designs or motifs such as soldiers, clowns or holly, or by personalizing them with names. To create a grand effect they would also add ornate trimmings of fringes, ribbon and velvet.

Elsewhere in the world, shoes are left out to be filled with gifts. In Holland children put their shoes in the chimney corner on 6 December and in Spain, at Epiphany, shoes are left on balconies and windowsills for the arrival of the Three Wise Men while in France wooden clogs or sabots are traditionally left on the hearth to be filled by the Infant Jesus on New Year's Day.

Gifts left in stockings or shoes are usually small and intended to keep children amused until later in the day when larger gifts are opened. In the nineteenth century, stockings would have been filled with 'penny toys' – nuts, fruit and sweets such as chocolate coins covered in gold paper. Larger family presents were left under the Christmas tree and opened later in the day after church and traditional Christmas lunch.

NEEDLEPOINT CHRISTMAS STOCKING

MATERIALS

Canvas: 40 × 55cm (16 × 22in)

Size 20 needle

Masking tape to bind edges

Appletons wool:

Pink 944	12m (13¼yds)
Red 995	50m (55yds)
Navy 747	6m (7yds)
Pale mauve 712	40m (44yds)
Dark mauve 715	30m (33yds)
Pale green 831	25m (28yds)
Dark green 834	105m (115yds)
White 991	45m (50yds)

Trace the initials from the sampler template on page 125. For this particular stocking, the initials have been enlarged slightly – this is not absolutely necessary, and they can easily be used direct from the alphabet sampler template. To work from a colour chart, remember that each square represents the intersection of the canvas and not the hole between the thread. Each square represents one tent stitch.

Additional festive sparkle can be added to a finished needlepoint stocking by sewing on tiny glass beads or pearls.

1. TENT STITCH (CONTINENTAL)

Continental tent stitch is worked with the needle held diagonally, but in horizontal or vertical rows to produce a thick ridge of yarn at the back of the mesh. It is hard-wearing, and tends not to distort canvas. Tent stitch is most suitable for use on items that will receive a lot of wear.

2. TENT STITCH (BASKET-WEAVE)

Basket-weave tent stitch produces a woven effect on the back of the canvas. It is quick to work and is recommended for filling in large background areas of colour. Like the continental stitch, you work one stitch to the right and under two threads of canvas, but cover the canvas diagonally. Work from the top-left hand corner of the canvas downwards concentrating on small blocks at a time.

When the needlepoint is completed, it is a good idea to back it with a strong fabric in a complementary colour. The same fabric should be used as a backing for the needlepoint and to provide the stocking lining. Suitable fabrics for this purpose include strong hessian, calico or satin. A plait made from surplus wool or wool of a contrasting colour should be attached to the back of the stocking in a long loop.

NEEDLEPOINT STITCHES

Details and instructions of stiches recommended for use when sewing the needlepoint stocking.

WHAT WILL GO INTO THE CHRISTMAS
STOCKING
WHILE THE CLOCK ON THE
MANTLEPIECE GOES TICK-TOCKING?
AN ORANGE, A PENNY,
SOME SWEETS, NOT TOO MANY,
A TRUMPET, A DOLLY,
A SPRIG OF RED HOLLY,
A BOOK AND A TOP
AND A GROCERY SHOP,
SOME BEADS IN A BOX,
AN ASS AND AN OX,
AND A LAMB, PLAIN AND GOOD,
ALL WHITTLED IN WOOD,
A WHITE SUGAR DOVE,
A HANDFUL OF LOVE,
AND IT'S VERY NEAR DONE –
A BIG SILVER STAR
ON TOP – THERE YOU ARE!
COME MORNING YOU'LL WAKE TO
THE CLOCK'S TICK-TOCKING
AND THAT'S WHAT YOU'LL FIND IN
THE CHRISTMAS STOCKING

Christmas Stocking
by Eleanor Farjeon

EDIBLE DECORATIONS

BEFORE METALLIC TINSEL AND shiny glass baubles were invented, many festive decorations were made from simple flour and water mixtures or basic biscuit recipes. Shapes were cut from rolled pastry, baked, decorated with paint and coloured paste, then varnished. In England and North America the basic salt-dough recipe used to make decorations is very simple. The dough can be sculpted or cut into many different shapes to hang on the Christmas tree including stars, angels, toys and trumpets.

In Germany the most common decorated biscuits are made from a type of gingerbread known as *Lebkuchen*, meaning life cakes. Traditionally they were much heavier than they are today and were full of dried fruit and energy-giving sugar, which is the probable explanation for their name. Large heart-shaped biscuits with messages piped in icing and bunches of bright marzipan flowers for decoration, are hung by colourful ribbons from doorknockers and fireplaces.

The city of Nuremberg in Germany has a 600-year-old tradition of cake-making. Nuremberg honey cakes, made with spices such as cardamom and aniseed as well as honey and lemon, are very much a part of a traditional German Christmas.

BIRD OF PEACE

Decorations need not be confined indoors. This biscuit bird made from a Lebkuchen recipe takes festivities further afield.

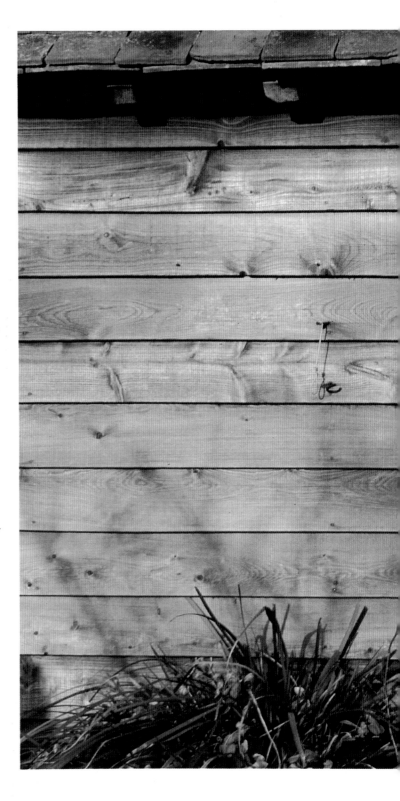

LEBKUCHEN TREE DECORATIONS

35g (1¹/₄oz) golden syrup
35g (1¹/₄oz) soft brown sugar
1 teaspoon black treacle
1 teaspoon water
A pinch of cinnamon
A pinch of mixed spice
A pinch of ground ginger
A pinch of nutmeg
50g (2oz) margarine
A pinch of bicarbonate of soda
A pinch of baking powder
100g (4oz) plain flour

Preheat the oven to 180°C (350°F, gas mark 4). In a pan, gently melt together the syrup, treacle, brown sugar, water and all the spices, stirring from time to time. Bring to the boil then remove from the heat immediately. Add the margarine, bicarbonate of soda and baking powder to the pan and stir until the fat has melted and the mixture is clear and smooth. Sieve the flour into a bowl, add the warmed syrup mixture then fold in the flour until a soft dough is formed.

On a floured surface, roll out the dough to an approximate thickness of 6mm (¹/₄in) and cut out your desired shapes (bells, stars, trees, etc.), remembering to make a small hole at the top of each shape large enough to allow ribbon or string to pass through. Arrange the biscuits on a buttered baking sheet and cook in the oven for ten minutes or until golden brown. They should be hard when cool.

STAR OF BETHLEHEM

A biscuit-base star edged with white icing makes a cheerful and inexpensive decoration to hang from the tree.

CHRISTMAS BELLS

Bells have long been associated with traditional Christmas festivities and their simple shapes make charming biscuits.

NUREMBERG HONEY CAKES

Makes 16

2 eggs
200g (7oz) icing sugar
3 tablespoons honey
3 tablespoons vanilla sugar (see below)
Zest of ¹/₂ lemon
1 teaspoon cinnamon
A pinch of ground cardamoms
A pinch of ground nutmeg
A pinch of ground cloves
¹/₂ teaspoon ground dried aniseed
75g (3oz) candied peel
175g (6oz) blanched ground almonds
250g (9oz) plain flour
1 tablespoon cornflour
1 teaspoon baking powder

Preheat the oven to 180°C (350°F, gas mark 4). To make the vanilla sugar, break a vanilla pod in half and place in a jar of caster sugar. Keep in a warm place for one-two weeks before use, shaking occasionally. Whisk the eggs, icing sugar, honey and vanilla sugar together until the mixture is thick and creamy. Stir in the lemon zest, spices, candied peel and ground almonds. Mix together the flour, cornflour and baking powder then sieve into the mixture and fold together. Place teaspoonfuls of the mixture on to non-stick baking parchment or a buttered baking tray and bake at 160°C (325°F, gas mark 3) for 15 minutes. Dredge lightly with caster sugar.

SALT-DOUGH

SMOOTH-FINISH RECIPE

2 cups plain flour
1 cup salt
A drop of cooking oil
Water

TEXTURED-FINISH RECIPE

2 cups wholemeal flour
2 cups salt
1 cup wallpaper paste
Water

Preheat the oven to 125°C (225°F, gas mark ¹/₂). Mix the flour, salt and oil together to form a dough, then add water, a little at a time, and knead repeatedly until a stiff dough is formed and all the air has escaped from the mixture – this prevents air bubbles from forming during baking. When the dough is ready, glaze it with egg white, then bake in the oven.

BASKET

Roll out the dough to a thickness of 6mm (¹/₄in) and, using a sharp knife, cut out a basket shape to the desired size. Cut out four strips of dough for horizontal slats and seven strips for verticals. Interlock horizontal and vertical slats to form a basket weave and lay the woven slats on top of the basket outline.

BASKET HANDLE

Roll out two long sausage shapes, join them together at one end and twist into a ring. Attach the handle to the top of the basket. If you intend to hang the finished

FRUIT BASKET

This bountiful basket made from a simple dough recipe will last for years. Spices such as cloves can be used to add detail.

decoration, remember to pierce a hole at the top of the handle to allow a hanging ribbon to pass through.

BASKET CONTENTS

Form the apples, pears and grapes by gently rolling the dough into balls and kneading into shape. Add cloves for a more realistic effect. To form the leaves, cut out leaf shapes and score across them lightly with a knife. Once you have made enough shapes for the basket, 'glue' them together using a watered down version of the dough. When the whole basket is assembled, glaze with egg white then bake in the oven.

TO MAKE BIRD OF PEACE

Cut out a bird shape from the dough and score fine lines to form a tail. Pierce a hole at the top of the decoration, large enough to house a strip of decorative ribbon.

EVERGREENS

LONG BEFORE THE CHRISTMAS tree became an established symbol of yuletide, branches of evergreen foliage were used in festive decoration. In Roman times laurel and bay were cut to form Saturnalia wreaths which were brought indoors for the celebration of the goddess Sternia. Because evergreens retained their leaves throughout the cold winter months, pagans held them as sacred symbols of good fortune, endowed with magical properties. Pagan associations with evergreen so shocked the Puritans that in 1647, officers were sent to a number of London churches, including Saint Margaret's opposite the Houses of Parliament, to remove all traces of it from the ecclesiastical environs.

The jagged points of the green holly leaf and its bright red berries are traditionally thought to make it a potently male plant, with the power to ward off witches. Others of a more Christian frame of mind say the berries represent drops of Christ's blood. The smooth leafed variegated holly and trailing ivy are associated with the female gender, but ivy is also linked with the wine-drinking god Bacchus and is said to protect against drunkenness.

Mistletoe was a plant worshipped by the pagans for its supposed powers of fertility, it was also used by Druids in their rituals. In many

UNDER THE MISTLETOE

An evergreen ball hanging in a doorway gives a festive welcome to visiting family and friends.

rural parts of England mistletoe is still not brought into the church, although in York Minster a bough is laid on the altar and left in place for the whole of the Christmas season. These days the most common custom still followed is the forfeit of a kiss by a girl or boy caught standing under an overhanging branch of mistletoe.

Wreaths were originally the centre-piece of festive decoration and came in a variety of shapes and forms. Kissing boughs created around hoops of wood or metal, shaped into a crown, were decorated with mistletoe and apples. Advent wreaths were made from branches of evergreen and adorned with four candles, one of which was lit on each Sunday in December leading up to Christmas Day when they were all lit together. Following a similar ritual, advent calendars or houses have a window opened each day during December to reveal a picture or sweet, although in Victorian times it would have been a moral motto or saying.

The introduction of the traditional Christmas tree is accredited to Queen Victoria's husband Prince Albert, although some records suggest that Queen Charlotte, wife of George III, had a tree at Windsor in the eighteenth century. Prince Albert certainly popularized the tree-dressing custom of his native country, erecting his first Christmas tree at Windsor Castle in 1841. The origins of the Christmas tree are believed to lie in the Paradise tree or Tree of Life, represented in medieval Creation plays. A manuscript dated 1605 chronicles a tree 'decorated with roses cut out of many coloured papers, apples, wafers, gold foil and sweets'. The use of candles and, latterly, electric lights is thought to portray the image of a starry and celestial heaven.

EVERGREEN RING

CHRISTMAS GREENERY

*Mistletoe is surrounded by tales and legends, many of which
are linked to the themes of fertility and magic.*

A POPULAR CHRISTMAS CAROL 'The Holly and the Ivy' can be seen as a reminder of Christ's life. The first verse points out *'The Holly and the Ivy, When they are both full-grown, Of all the trees that are in the wood, The holly bears the crown'*, the crown being symbolic of Christ the King of Heaven. The second verse recalls *'The holly bears the blossom, As white as lily flower, And Mary bore sweet Jesus, To be our sweet Saviour'*. The third verse turns to the holly's red berry — *'As red as any blood'* referring to the crucifixion, and the final verse highlights the holly's spiky leaf *'As sharp as any thorn, And Mary bore sweet Jesus Christ, On Christmas Day in the morn'*.

TO MAKE AN EVERGREEN HANGING BALL

This is a simple version of a traditional mistletoe and evergreen ball. The branches are simply tied together securely, rather than placed in florist's foam or moss. If kept in a cool place it will keep its freshness for a long time.

MATERIALS
5 or 6 good size branches of each of the following: mistletoe, ivy and holly. If these are difficult to find in quantity add branches of yew, pine, spruce or fir.

Gather together three or four stems of each variety of evergreen, so that the bunch is an evenly mixed group of all types. Tie the ends together securely and cut the stumps of the branches to a similar length. Locate the centre of the bunch, and through it tie decorative cord or gold rope. Hang the bunch up from a hook or peg and continue to add more, slightly shorter bunches, all around the hanging central mass. Secure the shorter bunches to the main one with loops of wire. Continue adding branches until the ball shape is achieved then cover the central tying point with a wrap of ornate fabric and a bow. Alternatively, wrap the arrangement with hand-printed paper.

THANKSGIVING

THANKSGIVING IS A TIME OF fun, feasting and family gatherings and survives as one of the most unspoilt and least commercial holidays in the North American calender. Thanksgiving is literally an occasion for 'giving thanks', commemorating the bringing-in of the first successful harvest planted by the settlers in the New World during the sixteenth century.

Today's Thanksgiving menu is based on the simple fare eaten at the first Thanksgiving meal. Dishes traditionally include turkey, corn bread made from indigenous maize, sweet potato and pumpkin pie. These days a number of different dishes may be added to the basic ones, reflecting the origins of the family hosting the meal but no matter what other embellishments are added, Thanksgiving lunch is a meal for all the family and as many as 25 or 30 people may attend.

Gifts are not exchanged at Thanksgiving, but as the numbers attending the meal tend to be large, it is customary to give the host a gift of food; perhaps a basket of nuts or some cheese. As alcoholic drinks are more associated with Christmas than with Thanksgiving, home-made cordials are often drunk with the meal and bottles of special fruit or berry drinks can be made and given.

The Thanksgiving meal is usually eaten at midday. Tables are traditionally covered with simple white cloths and decorated with candles and arrangements of autumnal dried flowers and leaves in shades of gold, red and brown – green is saved for Christmas decorations.

After lunch, which may go on for four or five hours, families often attend a church service. Traditionally, Thanksgiving celebrations were rounded off with family folk dances.

PUMPKIN PIE

For a 23cm (9in) pie shell:

PASTRY
175g (6oz) plain flour
1/2 teaspoon salt
1 tablespoon caster sugar
1 teaspoon baking powder
85g (3oz) unsalted butter
1 egg yolk
4 tablespoons double cream

FILLING
450g (1lb) cooked pumpkin (see below)
2 eggs slightly beaten
85g (3oz) brown sugar
1 1/2 teaspoons cinnamon
1/2 teaspoon ground nutmeg
1/2 teaspoon dry powdered ginger
A pinch of ground cloves
1/2 teaspoon salt
3 tablespoons molasses
420ml (1pt) evaporated milk

Preheat the oven to 200°C (400°F, gas mark 6). To make the pastry: sift the flour, sugar, salt and baking powder into a bowl. Rub in the butter until a fine breadcrumb-like consistency is produced. Lightly beat the cream and egg yolk together then add to the flour using a fork to mix it in. Turn the dough onto a floured surface and knead. Cover the dough and leave it in the fridge for 30 minutes. Remove and roll out to line a greased 23cm (9in) pie dish. Prick base and bake blind for 15 minutes.

THANKSGIVING PUMPKIN

The rich orange pulp of the pumpkin can be used to make soups and preserves, but for Thanksgiving it forms the base of the traditional pie. Left-over pastry can be cut into strips and made into a lattice.

For the filling: remove the pulp from the pumpkin and discard pips and stringy fibre. Cut flesh into pieces, cook in water until tender and allow to cool.

In a large bowl combine pumpkin, eggs, sugar, spices, salt, molasses and evaporated milk. Stir with a wooden spoon until mixture is smooth. Fill pie shell with pumpkin mixture then bake for 50 minutes or until the tip of a sharp knife inserted in the centre is clean when withdrawn. Serve warm.

FINISHING TOUCHES

WRAPPING AND PACKING IS AN INTEGRAL part of gift giving and sometimes a box can be a valuable present in its own right. A Pennsylvania Dutch bridegroom gave his wife-to-be a small oval painted 'bridesbox' in which to keep her hair ribbons and handkerchiefs. The wooden box was painted with traditional symbols such as pomegranates for fertility and doves for happiness, and was a treasured and enduring gift.

Crackers are now mostly confined to Christmas celebrations but they were originally used on many occasions such as Easter Sunday, weddings and anniversaries, although in the USA, crackers at Christmas are still not common-place.

'BROWN PAPER PACKAGES TIED UP WITH STRING,
THESE ARE A FEW OF MY FAVOURITE THINGS.'

The Sound of Music, Rodgers and Hammerstein

PRINTING PAPERS

BEFORE MECHANICAL PRINTING made it possible to buy wrapping paper by the roll, the paper used to wrap a gift could take as much time and effort to make as the gift itself. Hand-printed papers were, in the past, used in many ways; some old books had decorative end-papers, made from individually marbelled or patterned sheets, and even wallpaper was hand-printed.

But gift wrapping is not necessarily confined to paper. For smaller gifts a silk or printed cotton handkerchief could provide an interesting outer layer, and make an additional gift in itself. Cardboard boxes covered and lined with pretty materials or stencilled and painted wooden boxes are also attractive.

Using paper is probably amongst the quickest and cheapest ways of wrapping, but that does not mean that it has to be bland or boring. For an 'authentically' old-looking gift, a sheet of strong, white paper can be carefully aged by toasting it very lightly under a grill – taking great care not to set it alight. This lightly toasted paper has the appearance of velum or parchment and, when tied with red and gold ribbon held in place by drops of sealing wax, can look as though it has been around for centuries.

POTATO PRINTING

A simple way of printing a pattern onto paper is to use half a potato. Ensure that the potato is clean and mud-free, cut it in half, and then with a sharp knife cut away from the side of the potato leaving a raised block or shape. Rinse the cut potato in cool running water to remove the natural starch which may inhibit the ink or paint from taking to the surface. Press dry by stamping the potato on a tea-towel or blotting paper. To print, simply press the

WRAPPING IT UP

Plain papers can be transformed into special wrappings with simple, repeated print designs and messages.

cut potato edge into a saucer of paint or dye and lay carefully onto the sheet of paper. Tap the top firmly to make the print even, and lift off neatly. Interesting effects can be created by overprinting the same shape in different colours, or making a shadowy effect by over printing the second shape, off-centre from the first.

PASTE DECORATION

Another way to decorate paper is to use rice or cornflour-coloured paste into which a design can be scratched or drawn. Dissolve 50g (2oz) of rice flour into 50ml (2fl oz) of boiling water and stir until

smooth. When the paste is cool add paint or colouring. Using a wide decorator's paintbrush cover a sheet of paper with the coloured paste. While the paste is still wet trace on your design using a stick, nail, pastry roller or comb. Scratch your pattern into the paste just deeply enough so that a pale line appears. Choose a simple pattern such as a trellis or stripe, or an easy-to-repeat motif like a diamond or a square. Hang the paper up to dry before using it as a wrapping.

TIPS ON COVERING BOXES

When using an already printed box as a base, make sure that the print will not run when glue is put on it.

Test that the fabric or paper being used as a covering will not let the existing pattern show through.

When estimating the amount of paper or fabric needed to cover each area, overestimate rather than underestimate.

To make neat corners it is useful to have a book or block to lean the box against. Cut away excess material.

Double-sided tape is useful for attaching a paper covering onto a box. The tape is invisible but provides a secure binding.

Be careful when using staples through fabric. Make sure the staple passes right through the material and out the other side.

112

PAPER PLEASURES

*Hand-printed papers hang in the sunlight to dry. Varying
textures of paper react in different ways to inks and paints, and
wetting the sheet of paper with water before applying the
colour will give a soft effect.*

113

MAKING A PRESENTATION BOX

BASIC MATERIALS

Assemble the basic items – a wide and quite roughly bristled brush for painting; a piece of sturdy card, ribbon, string or elastic tape; a sharp knife or blade; a metal ruler for measuring and to cut against.

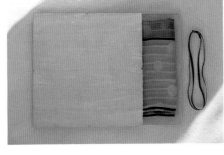

FOLDING AND WRAPPING

When all the sides are folded in and around the gift, secure them by placing a length of elastic tape, sewn together at the ends, from one side to the other. Repeat this with an identical piece of tape on the other sides.

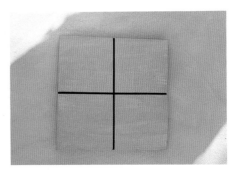

MEASURING AND MARKING

Measure and mark out the shape as shown then carefully score the card with the blade or knife. The cut should go through about two-thirds of the thickness of the card. This will make folding easier and give a neat finish.

MAKING A PRESENTATION BOX

MATERIALS

1 sheet of thick card
A blade or sharp knife
A length of ribbon
Metal ruler
Scissors

This simple box requires no adhesive tape or staples; it is a simple and attractive way of wrapping a gift, and the dimensions can be altered to suit any size of gift. The fold-over box is ideal for gifts of clothes, whether you are giving a silk scarf (to fit the dimensions given here) or a jumper for which a larger box is needed.

It is easy to create stylish and innovative packaging by applying paint effects and

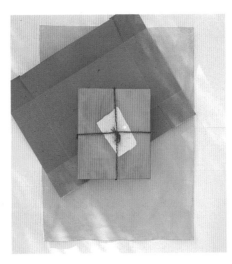

SEALING THE WRAPPING

The finished parcel may carry a hand-written note which can be held securely in place and decorated with a small blob of sealing wax in a contrasting colour.

decorations to plain card. In the photograph here, plain grey paper has been used as a base for a deep turquoise water colour wash. To achieve the same effect, apply paint roughly so that areas of grey show through the turquoise paint, to create a textural effect.

On the wrong side of the paper, draw in the lines where the paper will be folded. Using scissors, cut the corner and centre sections then deeply score the paper along the fold lines, being careful not to cut right through the paper.

Wrap your gift in tissue paper and lay it in the centre of what will be the base of the box. Pass a length of ribbon underneath from top to bottom, and another length from left to right.

Fold the sides of the box up around the gift, and fold the side flaps of the lid area inwards. Fold over and place the lid sides over the base sides. Carefully draw up the ribbons and tie neatly, but not so tightly that the box puckers.

DECORATING DEVICES

Plain wrappings make a perfect background to set off a special decoration such as a single rose. Keeping the other wrappings minimal highlights the shape of the bloom.

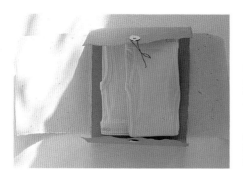

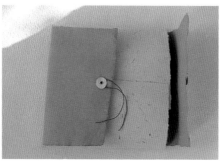

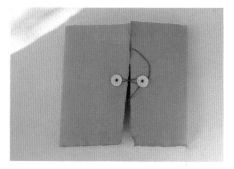

CREATING A GIFT BOX

Using two sheets of paper, one placed cross-wise on the other, enables you to make a box-like raised-side parcel, ideal for delicate gifts that may be crushed or wrinkled.

FOLDING THE SIDES

Fold the inner layers of paper over the gift so that they meet evenly in the centre. Repeat the action with the remaining layer of paper, and cover the open sides.

CLOSING THE BOX

A simple fastening can be made by attaching two cardboard discs with glue or tape. The cardboard could be substituted with buttons or decorative beads, and the sides tied firmly with ribbon.

CRACKERS

CELEBRATION CRACKERS

To make your own crackers you will need stiff card, decoration paper, double-sided tape and decorations of paper, fabric or dried flowers.

ASSEMBLING CRACKER TUBES

Place the two outer tubes 4cm (1¹/₂in) in from the edges of the paper and centre the middle tube. Secure the tubes using double-sided tape.

SECURING CRACKER ENDS

Take a piece of string and gently pull together the two ends to form a 'pull' at the end of the cracker. Secure with a piece of thin cord.

CRACKERS DATE BACK TO 1840, when Tom Smith, a baker and confectioner, was inspired by the decorative wrappings of French *bon bons* on a trip to Paris. On returning to his London shop he applied the same principle to his own products, adding a love message and later a snap and paper hat. So the cracker was born. It remained popular during the Victorian era as a means for commemorating all sorts of special occasions.

MATERIALS

1 piece of strong paper measuring 18cm (7¹/₄in) x 48cm (19in)

3 x thin pieces of card for inner tubes, each measuring 10.5cm (4¹/₂in) x 19cm (7¹/₂in).

Thin cord or string

Double-sided tape or glue

METHOD

Roll the three pieces of card for the inner tubes to a diameter of 5cm (2in), overlap

TRADITIONAL CRACKERS

Tom Smith, a London baker, invented crackers in the 1840s. This early box (above) shows the delighted recipient of some of Smith's innovative gifts.

ends and tape or glue together each tube. Position the three tubes along the bottom edge of a large piece of paper, with the middle tube centred on the paper. Each of the end tubes should be positioned 4cm (1¹/₂in) in from either edge of the paper. Stick the tubes to the paper with double-sided tape. Insert your gift and/or snap. Roll the paper around the card tubes, with an overlap of approximately 1cm (¹/₂in) and secure with double-sided tape.

Use a piece of string to wrap around one end of the middle tube, gently at first so as not to tear the outer paper. Once squeezed sufficiently, take away the cord and tie a tight knot with thin cord. Repeat for the other end and decorate the cracker. Glue the end tubes in place.

A BOX OF FEASTS

Finished crackers look extra special when embellished with a variety of decorations, including cinnamon sticks, dried flowers and textured papers. A simple box edged with decorative paper completes the effect.

TAGS AND LABELS

RIBBONS AND BOWS

Expensive satin ribbons and pieces of lace may add a hint of luxury to a gift but even cheap domestic trimmings can be made to look special. The textures of upholstery tape, webbing and string take on interesting effects when dyed.

Labels are an important part of a gift and can be made to match or contrast the gift wrapping. Left-over cuttings from a decorated box or the printed papers mentioned before could be used to make small envelopes (much favoured by the Victorians) to hold a small letter. Labels can be cut to reflect a seasonal shape, from a heart for Valentine's day, to an egg or fish for Easter and a pine tree for Christmas.

Geometric shapes can be created to complement the pattern or motif printed on the paper, or indeed the shape of the parcel itself. Borders drawn in ink or painted around the rim of the tag give it a finished look and colourful tapes, threaded through a small punched hole on the edge, can be used to tie it to the gift.

Dried leaves and petals also make attractive labels. Large chestnut leaves and good sized rose petals can be pressed between sheets of blotting paper until the sap has gone and they become paper-like. Use paint of a constrating colour and write on your message carefully as the leaf or petal may crack. Alternatively, write the message on a piece of paper and attach that to the leaf.

TAGS AND LABELS

Labels and tags can be made to match or compliment a wrapping. Cut-out shapes, dried flowers, snippets of lace and ribbon can all be used to personalize a card and make its message extra special.

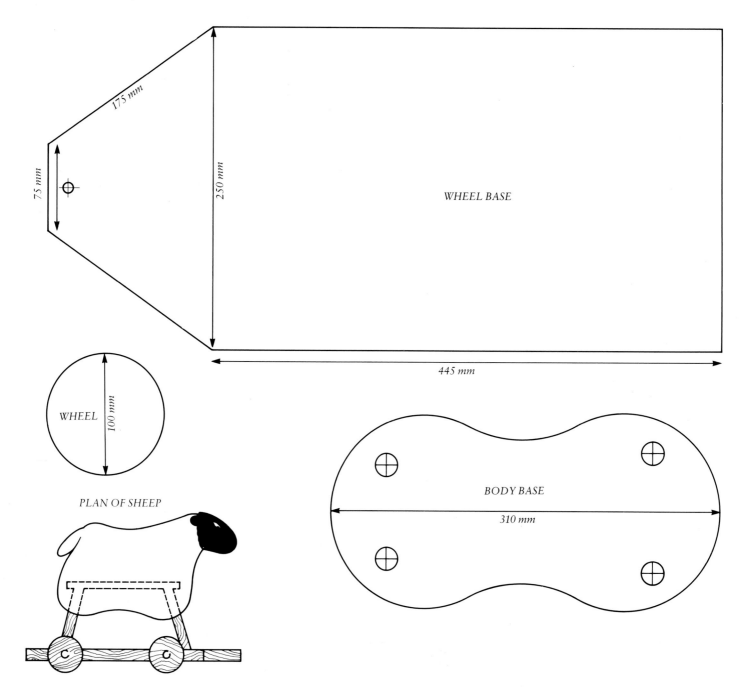

175 mm

75 mm

250 mm

WHEEL BASE

445 mm

100 mm

WHEEL

PLAN OF SHEEP

BODY BASE

310 mm

SHEEP ON WHEELS

Following the instructions given on pages 54 and 55, cut out the wooden shapes shown opposite and the fabric shapes on this page to create a delightful traditional toy.

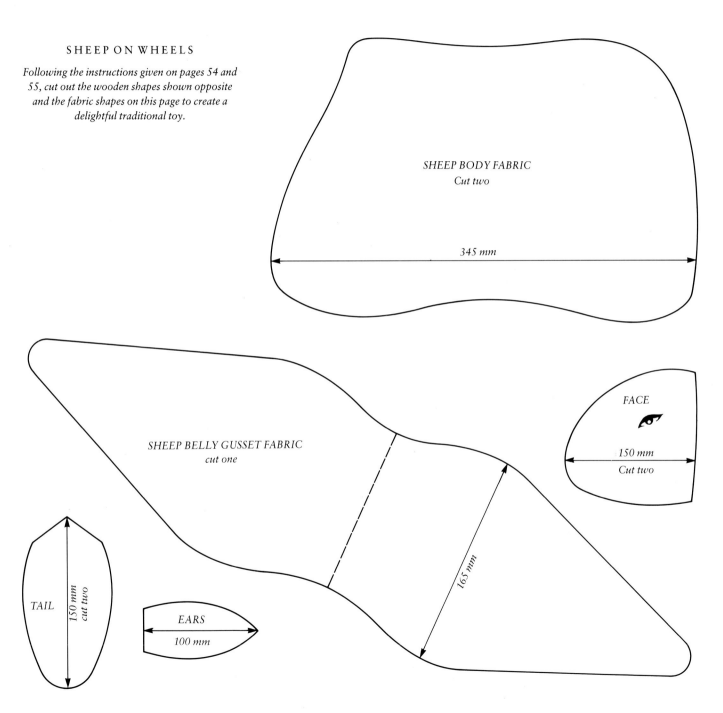

SHEEP BODY FABRIC
Cut two

345 mm

SHEEP BELLY GUSSET FABRIC
cut one

165 mm

FACE

150 mm
Cut two

TAIL

150 mm
cut two

EARS

100 mm

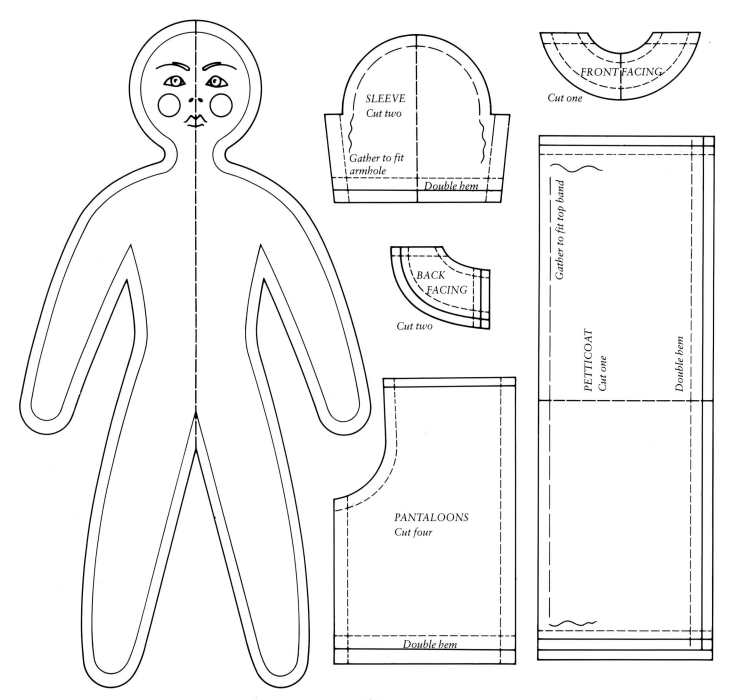

SLEEVE
Cut two

Gather to fit armhole

Double hem

FRONT FACING

Cut one

BACK FACING

Cut two

Gather to fit top band

PETTICOAT
Cut one

Double hem

PANTALOONS
Cut four

Double hem

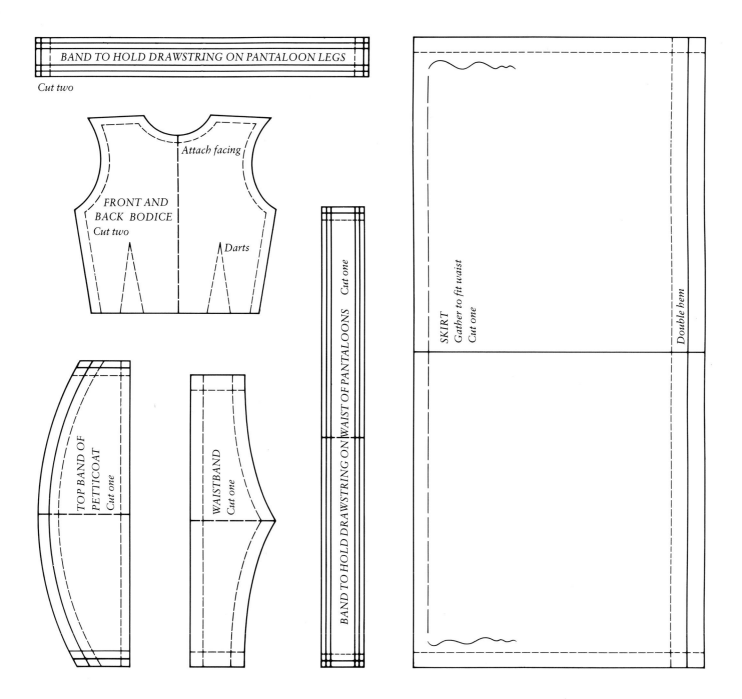

BAND TO HOLD DRAWSTRING ON PANTALOON LEGS

Cut two

FRONT AND
BACK BODICE
Cut two

Attach facing

Darts

TOP BAND OF
PETTICOAT
Cut one

WAISTBAND
Cut one

BAND TO HOLD DRAWSTRING ON WAIST OF PANTALOONS   Cut one

SKIRT
Gather to fit waist
Cut one

Double hem

CHRISTENING ROBE, BONNET AND BOOTEES

Use these templates and a sheet of graph paper to create your own paper pattern. For the christening robe skirt, you will need a piece of fabric 143cm × 69cm (52¹/₂in × 25¹/₂in). Sew together along edges and attach to bottom of front bodice, gathering fabric as you sew.

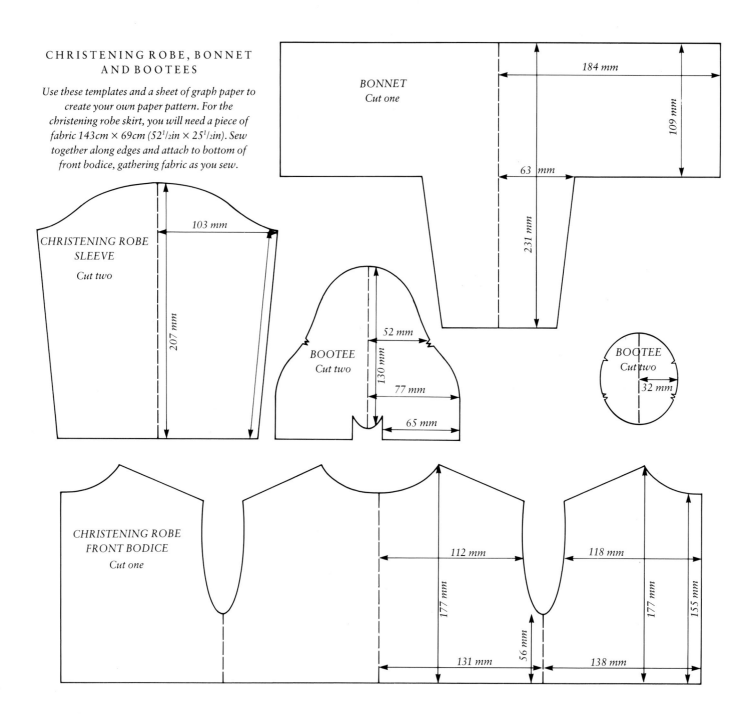

BONNET
Cut one

184 mm

109 mm

63 mm

231 mm

CHRISTENING ROBE
SLEEVE

Cut two

103 mm

207 mm

BOOTEE
Cut two

52 mm

130 mm

77 mm

65 mm

BOOTEE
Cut two

32 mm

CHRISTENING ROBE
FRONT BODICE

Cut one

112 mm

118 mm

177 mm

177 mm

155 mm

56 mm

131 mm

138 mm

A B C D E F
G H I J K L M
N O P Q R S T
U V W X Y Z

A B C D E F G H I J K L M N
O P Q R S T U V W X Y Z
1 2 3 4 5 6 7 8 9 0

INDEX

DIRECTORY/ACKNOWLEDGMENTS

OILS, PICKLES AND VINEGARS

English Provender Company Ltd
Aldreth
Cambridgeshire CB6 3PG
Maker of speciality foods from quality
ingredients and traditional recipes.

FLOWERS, WREATHS AND BULBS

Jane Packer
56 James Street
London W1
Original and classical flower design
and arrangements.

PAINTED ENAMELWARE

Len Skinner
c/o 64 Trenchard Road
Holyport
Nr Maidenhead
Berkshire SL 6 2LR
Traditional hand-painted narrow-boat
ware.

BABY'S QUILT

Damask Furnishings and Finery Ltd
Unit 10, Sulivan Enterprise Centre
Sulivan Road
London SW6 3BS
Designer and retailer of fine linens,
quilts and embroidered goods.

BABY CLOTHING AND LACE

Heirlooms Ltd
Unit 2, Arun Business Park
Bognor Regis
West Sussex PO22 9SX
Designers and makers of traditional
fine linens, cotton and lace accessories.

DOLLS, TOYS AND EMBROIDERY

Melanie Williams
Bronllys Castle, Bronllys
Powys LD3 0HL
Wales
Toy and object maker using papier
mâché, needlework and embroidery.

HOT CROSS BUNS AND SIMNEL CAKE

Anthony Drodge
White's Bakery
8 Church Street
Sidmouth, Devon
Specialists in celebration cakes, breads,
pastries and chocolate work.

NEEDLEPOINT SAMPLER AND STOCKING

Glorafilia
The Old Mill House
The Ridgeway
Mill Hill Village
London NW7 4EB
Needlepoint and tapestry specialists.

CHRISTMAS PUDDINGS

Bettys
1 Parliament Street
Harrogate
North Yorkshire HG1 2QU
Bakers, confectioners, chocolatiers, tea
importers and blenders, coffee roasters.

ACKNOWLEDGMENTS

*The publisher thanks the following
photographers and organizations for their kind
permission to reproduce the photographs in this
book: 3 Courtesy of 'Old-fashioned Floral Gift
Labels'; 6 inset The Hulton Picture Company;
8 Courtesy of 'Old-fashioned Floral Gift Labels';
8–9 Danish Folk Museum, Copenhagen/
Bridgeman Art Library; 10 Mary Evans Picture
Library; 11 Fine Art Photographic Library
(Galerie Berko); 12–13 Mary Evans Picture
Library; 14 Mary Evans Picture Library/Steve
Rumney Collection; 15 Mary Evans Picture
Library/Explorer; 16 The Robert Opie
Collection; 17 Fine Art Photographic Library;
32 Royal Institution of Cornwall (County
Museum, Truro); 38 The Hulton Picture
Company; 44 Ulster Folk & Transport Museum;
52 Victoria & Albert Museum, London/
Bridgeman Art Library; 58 Mary Evans Picture
Library; 64 Mary Evans Picture Library; 74
Mary Evans Picture Library; 80 Bridgeman Art
Library; 92 Mary Evans Picture Library; 96
Courtesy of 'Old-Fashioned Vignettes'; 116
below The Robert Opie Collection. Special
photography by Pia Tryde, styled by Jane
Newdick: 1–2, 6, 18–31, 33–36, 39–43, 45–51,
53–56, 59–63, 65–72, 75–79, 81–90, 93–95,
97, 100–119 (except 116 below).*

AUTHOR'S ACKNOWLEDGMENTS

*I would like to thank the staff of Conran
Octopus, in particular Joanna Bradshaw, Meryl
Lloyd and Sally Poole, and for their help and
support, Jane Newdick, Georgina Rhodes and
Pia Tryde; and Sandy Johnston for his patience,
advice and assistance.
Thanks to the following designers and makers:
Melanie Williams, Anne Parker, Jane Packer,
Len and Elizabeth Skinner, Gillian Lenfestey,
Carole Lazarus, Jennifer Berman, Sally Holme
and Betty's Bakery, Caroline Dunn, Anthony
Drodge and all at Heirlooms.
Also thanks to the following for their help: Conal
Walsh and company, Jane Bryant, Paddy and
Jean Johnston, Peggy Tucker, Debbie and Peter
Thompson, Elizabeth and Steven Small, Vicky
and Simon Young, The Leslie Bishop Company,
the British Library and Battersea Library.*